Contents

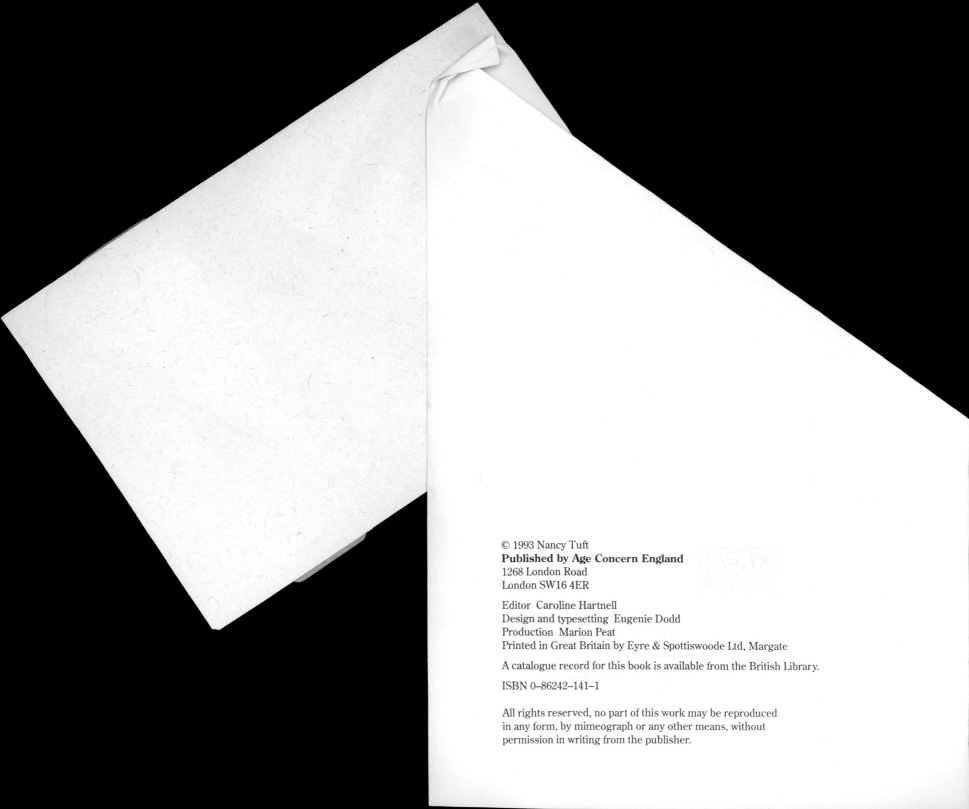

© 1993 Nancy Tuft
Published by Age Concern England
1268 London Road
London SW16 4ER

Editor Caroline Hartnell
Design and typesetting Eugenie Dodd
Production Marion Peat
Printed in Great Britain by Eyre & Spottiswoode Ltd, Margate

A catalogue record for this book is available from the British Library.

ISBN 0–86242–141–1

About the author

Nancy Tuft is an experienced author and journalist who specialises in writing for and about older people. Previous titles published by Age Concern include *Life in the Sun*, a guide to long-stay holidays and living abroad in retirement, *Looking Good, Feeling Good*, a challenging and positive look at the importance of style and personal appearance in later life, and *An Active Retirement*, for people adjusting to retirement who are seeking new ways to spend their time but are uncertain where to start.

She has tutored a series of retirement courses for Bromley Adult Education Service, as well as leading lifestyle sessions in seminars on retirement guidance.

Aged 60, with three adult children and five grandchildren, Nancy Tuft lives in Bromley where she is an active member of the local University of the Third Age.

Introduction

Most people enjoy a good day out, particularly if the arrangements are made by someone else. This book is aimed at that 'someone else', whether you are a professional group organiser or doing it on a voluntary basis.

Anyone can find themselves with an outing to organise, even if they have never done anything like it before. Many retired people belong to clubs or societies – a branch of U3A (University of the Third Age), the Pre-Retirement Association, ARP Over 50 or Probus; an organisation like the Women's Institute, Townswomen's Guild, British Legion or United Services Club with a lot of older members; a retired members' section of a company sports and social club, the local horticultural society or history society, and countless others. If you belong to a club, you may at some point be asked to organise the club outing.

But you do not have to belong to a club to organise an outing. You might, for example, agree to organise a church outing or a corporate outing for retired employees.

Outings have come a long way in recent years, with many new experiences being added to the traditional coach trip to the seaside. The farming industry, for example, has diversified into day tourism on a huge scale, while shopping is now viewed as a leisure activity in its own right, with day trips to France as well as local visits to factory shops and out-of-town discount parks.

Day tourism is in fact a highly competitive business, and older retired people are attractive customers. Not only do people over State Pension age represent almost one in five of the population, but older people are doubly welcome in that they often plan their outings at off-peak times, avoiding crowded weekends and bank holidays. Older customers help keep the turnstiles ticking over all the year round. Anyone responsible for arranging outings for older people is therefore a key figure in the business of day tourism. You should be able to pick and choose, comparing places and prices for value for money.

This book deals mainly with day outings, but it does also touch on overnight stops, and on the Package Travel Regulations which came into effect at the end of 1992 (see pp 75–76). Even a theatre visit which involves an overnight stop takes on a new dimension under the new Regulations. However, the book does not deal with longer breaks of two or three days; these are really short holidays rather than extended day trips.

The two crucial elements in organising a successful outing are choosing the right place to go and meticulous planning. This book aims to take you through all the different stages of organising an outing for older people. Chapter 1 summarises the main tasks – and attributes – of a group organiser. Chapter 2 looks at the whole process of deciding where to go, and at the organiser's role in gathering up information and presenting options to prospective members of the party. Chapter 3 makes suggestions for different sorts of outing. Chapter 4 looks at general planning, including making detailed arrangements and contingency plans, while Chapters 5–8 look specifically at helpers, transport, eating out, arranging an overnight stay, and insurance. Finally, Chapter 9 brings you to 'the big day' itself.

Arranging outings of any kind is a big responsibility, requiring much hard work and planning behind the scenes. But those who do the job are unanimous in emphasising that it is also enjoyable and rewarding, bringing a lot of pleasure to many people.

Nancy Tuft

1 The group organiser's role

The prime objective of the group organiser is to put together an outing which everyone will enjoy and remember with pleasure. As already indicated, the two crucial elements here are selecting an outing that suits all the members of your party and careful planning down to the last detail.

This chapter looks first at who the group organiser might be, the different settings they might be working in, and the possibility of having a co-organiser or deputy. It then outlines the various tasks of the group organiser, and suggests some of the personal qualities that might help the organiser in carrying out these tasks.

THE GROUP ORGANISER

A group organiser may be a professional person who organises outings as part of their job or someone working on a voluntary basis.

Particularly if you are a professional organiser, you may be much younger than the people who will be going on the outing (for example a staff member working in the personnel department of a company with a commitment to retirement welfare). Arranging outings may be only a small part of your job. Nevertheless, you will want your efforts to live up to the challenge of previous trips.

People who arrange club or society outings are likely to be volunteers; they are also likely to be members themselves – though probably among the more fit and active members. But you might not belong to a club or society at all. You might, for example, organise a church outing simply as someone who goes to a particular church.

Whether you are a professional or a volunteer organiser, you may well be operating under the umbrella of a larger agency, perhaps a local Age Concern group or a local authority department such as leisure services or social services. Age Well clubs, for example, are run by members themselves but with the guidance of a project leader, whose responsibilities usually involve organising outings. If you are organising a corporate outing, with coaches converging from different parts of the country, you may well be responsible only for part of the group.

Whoever you are organising an outing for, it is as well to remember that even within the same organisation there may be considerable differences between people in terms of tastes, income, age and health. Lone women are likely to be much less well off than single men or couples. Group members may be fit and active newly retired people or more frail elderly people who seldom get out and about on their own. Some people will be long-standing members of a club or society, while others only join one in later years, perhaps on the advice of a GP, relative or neighbour who is concerned about their social isolation, particularly after a bereavement.

Having a co-organiser

If you are asked to organise an outing you may at first be horrified at the idea, particularly if you have never done such a thing before. One possibility might be to take on the task jointly with someone else. Having a co-organiser obviously reduces the amount of time organising an outing will take, but possibly more importantly it shares the responsibility: with two people involved key tasks are less likely to be forgotten, and going off together to inspect prospective sites could make an enjoyable day out in itself.

Having a deputy

Even if you are happy to take on the role of organiser on your own, it may be wise to have a deputy organiser who knows what is going on and could take over at any time, for example if you are taken ill on the day, or if someone in your party has an accident and needs to be taken to hospital.

How much you need a deputy on the day may depend on the extent to which you would otherwise be solely responsible for the party. If you are organising the trip as a member of a committee, will any of your fellow committee members be going? Will there be paid members of staff or volunteer helpers going on the outing? You would not in any case want to find yourself in the situation of having no one else in the party who you felt would be able to go off and make a phone call or provide other back-up support.

Nominating one member of the party as your deputy could possibly cause bad feeling if you don't do it tactfully. It would in any case make sense to do it before the day itself so that the other person can be fully briefed by you in case you are ill on the day.

THE TASKS OF THE GROUP ORGANISER

Whoever you are, organising outings is a big responsibility, with lots of preparation needed behind the scenes, and the group organiser will have many different roles to play. The tasks of a group organiser include the following (it would be a rash person who claimed to offer an exhaustive list):

- to work out how decisions are to be made and your own role in this process – whether the group organiser is more of a facilitator or a leader will depend very much on who your party consists of;

- to consider what sort of outing prospective members of your party are likely to enjoy, bearing in mind their interests, their state of health, their income, and the likely availability of helpers (you will need to check out people's interests and special requirements first);

- to collect information on various ideas that seem to you suitable (including rough costings) and circulate it to everyone to read before a get-together;

- to arrange a meeting at which a shortlist of alternative outings and alternative dates is considered and decisions made;

- to make detailed plans and timetable for the day, including contingency plans in case the weather is bad or something else goes wrong;

- to make sure you have enough helpers for the trip you have chosen and that they all know what is expected of them;
- to arrange transport and meal stops, and an overnight stay if necessary;
- to make sure insurance cover is adequate;
- to finalise numbers and collect people's contributions;
- to make sure everyone concerned is clear about the final arrangements for the day;
- to ensure you have everything you need to hand on the day itself.

Something that is useful to sort out at a very early stage is how often you are going to meet with your group, what you hope to achieve at each meeting, and what you will need to have found out before each meeting in order to make that possible. If you are organising a trip for a group that meets often – perhaps weekly – or if the outing is an annual event and so planned a long time ahead, you will probably be able to have as many meetings with your group as you want. Your timetable might then look something like this:

Preliminary meeting to get initial ideas and find out what people's interests/limitations/special requirements are. Nothing for you to find out before this meeting.

Second meeting at which venue and date are selected. You will need to have researched various options before this, including costs and access, and either circulated people with information in advance or brought it along to the meeting.

Third meeting at which details of meal stops, contingency arrangements for a rainy day, etc, are agreed on. You will need to have researched all the possible options before this.

Final meeting at which all arrangements are confirmed.

The timetable will obviously be different for each group. If you organise regular outings for a particular group of people, you will already have at your fingertips all the information that might have been elicited at a preliminary meeting. The major decision about where to go and the decisions on detail could be made at one meeting rather than two, provided you have done sufficient research beforehand. Here again, if you organise regular outings for a group you will already know, for example, that people enjoy stopping at a pub on the way. The information about final arrangements could obviously be put in a newsletter or special mailing – in fact, it's vital to put it all in writing even if you do have a final meeting.

THE QUALITIES A GROUP ORGANISER NEEDS

To achieve all this you will need to be efficient, imaginative, sensitive to people's needs, firm once decisions are made. You will also need to be a business-minded tour operator (budget-conscious, comparing prices and places for value for money), an efficient finance controller (keeping track of contributions, deposits and bookings), and a good team manager (liaising smoothly with committee members, helpers or paid staff). Above all, you will need to be able to relax on the day and enjoy the outing along with everyone else. If you are tense and anxious, this is likely to communicate itself to the rest of the party.

This may sound more like a description of Superwoman or Superman than an ordinary human being; in reality no one person is likely to combine all these qualities in equal measure. Most people will be better at some aspects of the job than others, but will nevertheless cope with the task as a whole.

One real advantage in having a co-organiser is that two people are likely to bring different personal qualities to the task: together you may come to resemble the Superman or Superwoman described above.

2 Deciding where to go

Deciding where to go is probably the key stage in organising a successful outing. Choosing the right place obviously doesn't lessen the importance of careful planning, but no amount of careful planning can make a good day out if the chosen trip isn't really suitable for the people who are going on it.

To recap from Chapter 1, the tasks of the group organiser at this stage are as follows:

- to consider what sort of outing prospective members of your party are likely to enjoy;
- to collect information on various ideas and circulate it to everyone to read;
- to arrange a meeting at which alternative outings and dates are considered and a decision is made.

This chapter takes you through the various stages in coming to a decision about where to go for your outing. Chapter 3 then looks at the different sorts of venue you might choose.

CHECKING OUT PEOPLE'S INTERESTS AND NEEDS

As suggested on page 11, if you have not organised a trip for a particular group of people before, it is worth holding a preliminary meeting to get some initial ideas and find out what people's interests/limitations/special requirements are, and what sort of outing is likely to suit them.

If you organise regular trips for a group, you should have this sort of information already, and you may just need to check up on anyone who is new to the group or who has not been on an outing before.

If the people who are going on the outing do not belong to a group that meets regularly, or they belong to a group that meets fairly infrequently and getting people to come out to an extra meeting is difficult, you could send all prospective party members a questionnaire. This could include questions on:

- suggestions for the proposed trip (to include anything that people like the idea of, however unlikely it might seem);
- people's interests/hobbies/leisure activities;
- previous outings people have been on and enjoyed (or not enjoyed);
- any problems with mobility (uses wheelchair; can only walk limited distance; needs help getting on and off coach, etc);
- any special dietary requirements (vegetarian, diabetic, etc);
- any other restrictions (eg someone gets tired easily, in which case a relatively short outing might be preferred; toilet on coach or frequent stops needed);
- if there is to be an overnight stop, whether people have any special requirements or preferences (must have toilet en suite or very near room; can't manage many stairs; must have single room, etc);
- financial limitations (people may not be able to pay more than a certain amount for an outing – it may be easier for people to admit this in a questionnaire than in a meeting);
- possible dates.

Once you have gathered together information of this sort, you will be able to eliminate certain types of venue immediately – because too many people have been there already or no one would be interested, or because it lacks wheelchair access or would take too long to get there. This should prevent you wasting a lot of time researching unsuitable venues.

It is obviously important to find an outing that is within the price range that prospective party members can afford. Some outings may simply work out too expensive. If there are just one or two people who couldn't afford a particular trip, you may be able to make special arrangements to enable them to go, as discussed on page 43.

Pat 'It's a bit like gardening. You put in a lot of preparation and groundwork. But that's how you find out what people's interests are and then you look around for attractions that match up.'

Don't be too disappointed if people do not come up with much in the way of constructive suggestions for venues. There are many possible reasons for this, as discussed on pages 16–17. It doesn't mean that they're not interested.

Beware, too, of restricting the choice of venue on the basis of your own preconceived ideas about what people would or would not like. A concert may not be a good choice for a group outing simply because it is difficult to cater for everyone's tastes. (Having said that, people will often go on a group outing and enjoy themselves at an event they would never have gone to as an individual.) But it is quite another matter to dismiss an 'educational' visit, say to a museum, as being too 'highbrow' for your group. Organisers can unwittingly impose their own limitations on other members of the party.

If people really aren't interested

If, on the other hand, you belong to a group that always has difficulty 'filling the coach' for the annual trip, which people go on mainly out of loyalty to the organiser who does so much hard work, it may be time to call it a day. If most people in the group own their own cars, it may be that outings are no longer the rare treat they were in the days before mass car ownership.

It may just be that a rethink is needed. A horticultural society, for example, may always have concentrated on spring, summer and autumn visits to flower shows. Suggesting a completely different sort of outing, not necessarily connected with gardening, could revive people's enthusiasm, as well as providing somewhere to go in the winter.

PEOPLE'S OWN SUGGESTIONS FOR VENUES

Suggestions from prospective party members about venues can be useful. However, an enjoyable experience of an individual visit with friends or family does not necessarily mean that the venue is a good choice for a group outing. Any venue will need checking out, preferably in person, to make sure there are appropriate group facilities (for example a large enough cafe or restaurant, plus alternative attractions in case of bad weather if the venue is an outdoor one). It is easier for a small family party in a car to move on somewhere else if the venue turns out disappointing than for a coach party.

Often group organisers feel let down if people don't come up with much in the way of suggestions for outings. If people seem content to leave everything to the organiser or a social committee, it may be partly because previous trips haven't been all that varied, and they have little basis for comparisons on which to make choices. Their experience may be limited mainly to traditional seaside outings.

People's horizons may also be restricted through lack of mobility and/or lack of access to information sources, such as tourist offices and the reference sections of public libraries. This is why it is so important for the organiser to act as a go-between, passing on as much information as possible before choices are made.

Cultural attitudes can also be a factor. For example, many older women still feel duty-bound to be home in time to prepare their husband's tea.

Group organiser 'I wondered why I was always being asked what time we'd be back. If I said anything much later than five o'clock or so they'd all start getting anxious. Then one day it dawned on me. I felt like saying, "Why on earth can't he get his own tea for once?" but I managed to hold my tongue. I did suggest that husbands were always welcome to come along too. But the men – those that were married, that is – seemed to think the club was just a women's thing. And that seemed to be how the women wanted it.'

In all these cases people may just need a bit of gentle encouragement to make suggestions. This is obviously only possible if you have a preliminary meeting – it is difficult to be encouraging in a questionnaire.

If people produce lots of promising ideas for outings, your role as an organiser may be mainly to look into these and come up with some hard information. Even so it is always worth doing some research into other possibilities, as you may think of something people like better.

If people haven't made suggestions, it will be up to you to come up with ideas and information. But even if they haven't had much input at the ideas stage, people may well become enthusiastic and involved when it comes to discussing the alternatives you suggest.

GATHERING INFORMATION

Once you have armed yourself with all possible information about people's wishes, interests and needs, it is time to start gathering up information about venues that might suit your party.

Remember that there is a big difference between glossy, image-creating leaflets aimed to appeal to individual tourists, and the more in-depth, hard information required by the organiser of outings. Don't be put off by any publication calling itself a travel trade manual, which is a group guide by any other name. Budget restraints may prevent you from buying too many annual guides and reference books, but these are usually available for reference in the public library.

Some good sources of information are listed below.

Tourist boards, national and regional, and local tourist information centres provide consumer leaflets and group information on attractions in their area (addresses of the main regional tourist boards are on pp 85–87).

Individual tourist attractions produce consumer leaflets; some produce videos for group organisers, and many offer free facility visits (for organisers to check out the venue). Take advantage of these if you have time. There is no substitute for first-hand knowledge. (It is always worth recording the details for future reference.)

Local authority leisure departments are becoming increasingly publicity-conscious, and most counties now produce guides intended to help encourage group visits. The London Tourist Board's publication *London for the Travel Trade* is particularly useful for any group organiser bringing a party into the capital. It lists attractions that are free, those which accept credit card bookings, group rates, and eating places. It also gives a map showing tourist coach parks.

Specialist books and guides, for example on museums or on gardens that are open to the public. (See pp 88–90 for suggested titles. These can be bought or looked at in the reference section of the public library.)

Group Travel Organiser is a monthly magazine (details on p 89), a key resource for group organisers. Copies may be sent free of charge to nominated organisers of regular outings. You can become a member of the GTO Association, which has local branches; one of the benefits of membership is free facility trips. You also get the chance to meet others and compare notes: there is still no substitute for personal recommendations.

Coaches Welcome is another free annual publication (details on p 88). It has county-by-county listings of tourist attractions particularly suitable for coach parties and useful information concerning meal stops. Many entries are privately run hotels, which are not part of major chains, and which cater for overnight stops.

Magazines and newspapers, national and local. Look out for articles on day tourism and advertisements in the ordinary press.

Travel and trade fairs, national or regional, for ideas, group travel promotions, and contacts for facility visits.

Mailing lists of theatres, museums, exhibition organisers, tour operators, coach companies, etc, for advance information on forthcoming events.

Senior citizens clubs sometimes produce an annual guide, with sections on places to visit, places to eat, local coach companies and holiday organisations, and so on.

When you've identified a few possibilities, you should send for and study specific information about possible venues. (If you're rescuing existing material from a previous file, make sure all the information is absolutely up to date and accurate.) At this stage you will want to:

- compare admission charges, concessions and group rates, catering facilities, etc. Minimum numbers for party rates will vary;

- get comparable quotes for transport;

- check how much deposit has to be paid and when, and if credit card bookings are accepted. You may want to raise your credit limit.

If at all possible, it is always a good idea to go to a proposed venue and have a good look round at first hand. You will then be able to see for your-self what the facilities are and whether they match the needs and/or expectations of your members. This is a much more reliable way of finding out what a place is really like than reading a brochure that is intended to make it sound attractive. It will also put you in a much better position to answer people's questions about the venue. As already men-tioned, many places offer free facility trips for group organisers.

Information on facilities for disabled people

Facilities for disabled people on day outings are improving all the time. The English Tourist Board's National Accessible Scheme with its green symbol, currently displayed by wheelchair-accessible holiday accommo-dation, will soon be extended to cover daytime visitor attractions. There are three categories of accessibility:

Category 1 Accessible to an independent wheelchair user.

Category 2 Accessible to a wheelchair user with assistance.

Category 3 Accessible to a wheelchair user able to walk a few paces and up at least three steps.

Useful specialist information sources for disabled people include the fol-lowing:

RADAR access guides to sports centres, museums, arts centres and other venues. Write to the Royal Society for Disability and Rehabilitation (RADAR – address on p 85) for their publications list.

Information for Visitors with Disabilities is a booklet published by the National Trust (address on p 84), whose adviser on access for disabled visitors is available to answer general enquiries. At many of the Trust's historic houses and gardens, there are manual wheelchairs, ramps, lifts and powered self-drive or volunteer-driven vehicles such as golf-type buggies.

A Guide for Disabled Visitors is a similar booklet published by English Heritage (address on p 83).

Places that Care (details on p 90) is a well-researched specialist publication describing many interesting and unusual day tourist venues, listed county by county. Symbols are used to describe access facilities.

Specific enquiries about facilities for disabled people should always be made to the intended site for an outing.

OTHER FACTORS TO BEAR IN MIND

The time of year

With certain outings it is the time of year that is the deciding factor. The annual 'blossom run', for example – a popular coach tour of the Kent apple and cherry orchards – is an obvious spring event. Evening outings to see the illuminations at Blackpool and Morecambe are traditionally outings for autumn when it begins to get dark earlier. Going to a firework display is an option for an outing in early November – an increasing number of displays are taking place each year.

Christmas events, too, are obviously seasonal, involving not only pantomimes and carol concerts but also many visitor attractions where special events are arranged in order to bring in more winter visitors.

Where events are held only once a year, a regular group organiser may like to check on this year's event for suitability in preparation for making arrangements for a group visit the following year.

The need to book ahead

Sometimes it is necessary to make early decisions because of the need to book well in advance. Many theatre bookings, for example, need to be made as much as 12 months in advance, so going to a popular show in a large group might not be a viable option for a trip that is being arranged only a month or two ahead. If you want to book a restaurant around Christmas, you will probably need to book well ahead. Basically, the larger the party the further ahead you should book.

Ideal length of the outing

Being tired makes everything less enjoyable; there is no point in spoiling the day by wearing people out. An afternoon outing can be as enjoyable as a whole day out, especially if much of the day is spent getting there and back. In addition, some group organisers need to gear outings to fit neatly within the weekday hours of a day centre or afternoon club session. This is quite common where members are picked up and taken home by regular transport.

What you will be looking for here are suitable places, both indoor and outdoor, within a strictly limited radius because of the time factor. With the recent growth in day tourism, there should be a reasonable choice of places of interest within easy distance of almost everyone.

An afternoon spent at a local library, or sitting in the park on a sunny afternoon, may not seem particularly exciting to you. But little trips like this may be much appreciated by less mobile people or by someone who has been a carer for a number of years and unable to get out of the house. In that case even a trip to the nearby town may be quite an adventure, particularly in areas where the local bus services have been cut.

Weekday or weekend?

Although weekday outings have the advantage of being 'off-peak', which means tourist places are likely to be less crowded and possibly cheaper to visit, there are also compelling arguments in favour of weekend outings. Coventry Age Concern, who own their own coach, quote the ready availability of working relatives who are free to act as helpers and escorts at the weekend, while an Age Well organiser in an inner city area commented that Sunday is often the loneliest day for people living on their own. 'The Sunday outings are easily the most popular.'

MAKING THE DECISION

Even if you have communicated with prospective party members entirely by post so far (newsletter, special mailing, questionnaire), it is a good idea to have a meeting to discuss your suggestions and make a final decision about where to go and when.

Make sure you obtain sufficient leaflets about the venue or venues you are suggesting for everyone to have one, and photocopy relevant extracts from available tourist material. Ideally people should see these before the meeting, but you can always pass leaflets and other information round at the beginning instead.

How much information do people need?

If you are going to put forward several alternative suggestions, you obviously won't want to spend time researching the real minutiae. You won't, for example, want to go to the trouble of getting possible menus for a pub lunch stop when you don't even know where you are going or what route you will be taking, let alone whether people want to stop at a pub for lunch. Nevertheless, there are certain things people will need to know before they can make any sensible decision:

- how long it takes to get there and back;
- likely setting off and arriving home times;
- how much the outing is likely to cost (getting into the attraction, transport, etc). This may be difficult to work out if you don't know how many people will be coming: a 53-seater coach, for example, will cost considerably less per head than a much smaller one or a minibus;
- what facilities are available (cafes, restaurants, shops, etc);
- how good access and facilities are for disabled people or people with limited mobility;
- what date(s) you are proposing.

You will also need to check how far in advance you need to make group bookings.

Discussing the options

It is a good idea to ask whether any of the group have visited the suggested venue and what they thought of it. There will always be someone who responds along the lines of 'Been there, done that, got the T-shirt'. However, it's worth reminding people that locations are constantly updating their attractions.

Fixing a date is almost always difficult, even if you put forward several alternatives. Whatever date you finally choose, there is likely to be someone who can't go on that day.

Something that new organisers in particular have to learn is that you are never going to please everyone. There is always likely to be someone who doesn't want to go to the place that is eventually chosen, or who is unhappy about the arrangements.

Group organiser 'Nothing was ever right. The seats wouldn't recline properly; the stops weren't long enough; if it wasn't too hot, there was a draught. You mention it, they moaned about it.'

The main thing is not to let such people get you down. Often the organiser will find that the rest of the party sits on them before long. If most people end up having an enjoyable day, you will have done your job well.

3 Theme trips and other outings

The range of attractions that you could visit on a day out has increased enormously in recent years. Organising visits around 'themes' is something that has gained in popularity. While some attractions – for example shire horse centres, steam railways and mining museums – exploit the nostalgia that is often felt for the past, others such as the Thames Barrier and nuclear power station visitor centres focus on the most up-to-date technology. A craft centre, a flower show, a garden or stately home, a museum or gallery, a theatre or concert, a factory shop or discount shopping park, a race meeting or country walk – these are just some of the possibilities for a day (or evening) out. Alternatively, your outing could just consist of arranging transport to and from an interesting place – or even your nearest town if you live in a rural area with little or no public transport.

This chapter describes these and many other suggestions for a day out.

Gardens and flower shows

Gardening is one of the most popular hobbies in retirement. Major events such as the annual Hampton Court Flower Show or the flower shows at Shrewsbury and Southport attract huge numbers of visitors. There are also local agricultural and horticultural shows.

If you are interested in gardening, or simply enjoy visiting gardens, the Royal Botanical Gardens at Kew, London; the Royal Horticultural Society (RHS) gardens at Wisley (Surrey), Pershore (Worcestershire), Rosemoor (Devon) and Ness (Cheshire); and the National Centre for Organic Gardening at Ryton-on-Dunsmore, Coventry, are all obvious attractions.

For details of their gardens and flower shows, write to the RHS at the address on page 84.

The annual publication *Gardens of England and Wales* (details on p 88) contains county-by-county listings of gardens open to the public, along with travel directions and details of facilities such as refreshments and wheelchair access. Many belong to the National Trust and are described in the *National Trust Gardens Handbook* (details on p 89). Groups are welcome by prior arrangement.

Historic houses and other buildings

Going round historic houses and stately homes is another popular activity. Some of the gardens listed in *Gardens of England and Wales* will also have a house that is open to the public. Other sources of ideas are the *National Trust Historic Houses Handbook* (details on p 89), which describes all Trust houses open to the public, and the *Guide to English Heritage Properties*. English Heritage properties include castles, ruins and other ancient monuments such as Stonehenge and Tintern Abbey as well as historic houses. The regional tourist boards and local tourist information centres should have information about houses in their areas.

Often houses where a famous person lived or was born are open to the public, and sometimes made into small museums. Examples are the Brontë Parsonage Museum at Haworth, West Yorkshire; Eastwood, near Nottingham, birthplace of D H Lawrence; and Thomas Hardy's house near Dorchester, Dorset.

Keeping up to date with modern technology

Two attractions which feature unique constructions on a national scale are the Thames Barrier and Eurotunnel, both of which have visitor centres. If you are interested in visiting a power station, Sellafield in Cumbria is probably the best known, but Nuclear Electric has ten purpose-built information centres open to the public showing how electricity will be generated in the 21st century.

A less likely-sounding option is a trip to the local sewage works. As improvements are made to sewage treatment, so shareholders and customers of the ten big water companies in England and Wales are being invited to tour their local sewage works. There has even been a national sewage week to promote such trips. A guided tour usually takes around half an hour.

This Modern World is the name of a U3A group in Bromley, Kent, specifically aimed at keeping members up to date with technological progress. Newspaper production; goods deliveries and stocking the shelves at the supermarket; the sorting of letters by the Royal Mail – these are all examples of talks and visits 'behind the scenes'.

Museums featuring past ways of life

Among the many 'how we lived then' attractions available are industrial, dockyard and mining museums all over the country. Beamish North of England Open Air Museum, near Chester le Street, Durham, includes a colliery village complete with chapel and school, shops, a working farm, and a railway station with steam locomotives, all illustrating life at the turn of the century. It is a recent winner of the European and British Museum of the Year award.

One place that will take everyone right back to childhood is the Museum of Advertising and Packaging run by Robert Opie in Gloucester. Opie has been called a shopping basket historian, with his unique collection of bottles, tins and cardboard cartons plus other advertising ephemera from Victorian times to the present day. Remember products like Rinso, Virol and Sunlight Soap? Many products, such as Colman's Mustard, Fairy Liquid and Bovril, are still going strong today, and it's fascinating to see the subtle changes in graphic design over the years.

Farms and shire horse centres

Farms specialising in 'day tourism' attractions will be listed in local tourist guides. Many feature demonstrations of rural activities such as cheese-making and the rearing of rare breeds of animals.

Londoners who remember the annual hop-picking exodus into Kent may enjoy trips to the Whitbread Hop Farm at Paddock Wood where, as well as the Victorian oast houses, there are the famous Whitbread shire horses.

Shire horses are a popular attraction in other parts of the country too. Norfolk has its own Shire Horse Centre in West Runton; at the Bradford Industrial Museum shire horses can be seen still earning their keep pulling trams and canal barges.

Fit and active older people may enjoy picking strawberries and other fruit and vegetables. The Farm Shop and Pick Your Own Association (address on p 83) publishes a free booklet listing farm shops and 'pick your own' sites throughout the country.

Steam railways

Attractions featuring earlier forms of transport always seem to be popular. Many local steam railways are preserved and run by devoted volunteers. They are featured in tourist guides all over the country, and are often popularly known by picturesque names such as the Primrose Line at Buckfastleigh, South Devon, or the Watercress Line at Alresford, Hants. One of the prettiest is the Tallylyn Railway in Gwynedd, running through beautiful Welsh countryside. As well as their normal service, most of these railways have specific dates set aside when disabled people are particularly welcome.

Anniversary events

Special exhibitions and events are often organised for centenaries or other important anniversaries. In 1994, for example, the 50th anniversary of D-Day, people will have countless opportunities to relive wartime history. At Duxford Airfield, an outpost of the Imperial War Museum in Cambridgeshire, visitors will be able to 'fly' in a Battle of Britain dogfight. There will also be re-creations of the domestic experience – air raids, food rationing, and working in munitions factories. The majority of military museums tend to be concentrated in the south-east, with the coastal towns of Dover and Portsmouth organising special attractions. An events list is available from the Southern Tourist Board (address on p 86).

Crafts exhibitions

Anyone who enjoys knitting, sewing or embroidery, or who has worked in the garment-making industry, might enjoy a visit to one of the regular exhibitions – Sewing for Pleasure, Creative Stitches and Crafts Alive – organised by a company called International Craft and Hobby Fair (ICHF). You can write to the address on page 84 for leaflets about forthcoming events. There are concessions for advance bookings and for parties.

Unlike many craft fairs, Crafts Alive events include live demonstrations by glass-blowers, blacksmiths, leather workers, potters, basket-makers, thatchers, etc.

Museums and galleries

Many larger museums and galleries now have education departments where you can make initial enquiries regarding a group visit. You may be allocated a special guide to show your party round.

Some visits benefit greatly from preparation by way of prior introduction to the subject-matter. It may be possible for a museum speaker, possibly someone from the Friends' Association, to come along and talk to your group first, bringing along slides and other interesting items. Specific examples where this can be arranged are the Black Country Museum at Dudley, West Midlands; the Ironbridge Gorge Museum, at Telford, Shropshire, and the Whitworth Art Gallery, at the University of Manchester.

If you are visiting a large city museum or gallery and it is likely to be a first visit for many members of your party, it may be a good idea to focus on one particular collection of exhibits or paintings rather than roaming superficially around the entire building.

To find out what is on offer in your area, see the annual publication *Museums and Galleries of Great Britain* (details on p 89).

Factory shops and tours

A guided tour round a factory, mill or pottery makes an interesting outing, with the added bonus of a visit to the factory shop and a chance to buy seconds, samples and/or surplus stock at discount prices.

As a change from seeing how items such as glassware, pottery and clothing are made, you could watch the preparation of cosmetics and skincare products at Bodyshop in Littlehampton, East Sussex. Or you could experience the sights and smells of a Grimsby kipper factory, a family-run business on the docks that specialises in fish smoking. Admission is free and visitors can buy produce such as smoked haddock fillets and smoked Scotch salmon in the wholesale shop afterwards.

A *Factory Shop Guide* (details on p 88) covering your region will give information on what factory shops there are, when they open and what they sell. It also lists factories which offer conducted tours. Groups should always book in advance for these. The guide also covers toilet availability and wheelchair access plus detailed travel directions, since many factories are off the beaten track and not easily accessible by public transport.

Indoor shopping centres

Indoor shopping centres that house branches of Boots, Marks & Spencer and other chain stores, plus a variety of smaller shops, usually have cafes and convenient toilets as well. Some of the larger purpose-built shopping centres, such as MetroCentre in Gateshead; Cwmbran Shopping near Newport, South Wales; and Thurrock Lakeside in Essex, include entertainments such as cinema, bowling and bingo. The newly furbished Buttermarket in Ipswich holds tea dances. Centres like these welcome groups. Coach parking is no problem, though some require prior notice.

Some of these shopping centres feature 'Shopmobility', a scheme whereby a limited number of self-operated powered wheelchairs and booster scooters are available on loan for people with walking difficulties. Pre-booking is advisable and a refundable deposit may be required.

Discount shopping parks

One of the first-ever discount shopping parks to be opened in Britain was the Hornsea Freeport Shopping Village, near Bridlington, Humberside. It offers clothing of well-known makes at cut prices; the 28-acre site includes branches of Aquascutum, Austin Reed, Laura Ashley and many more.

Clarks Village is a new factory shopping complex in Street, Somerset, with lots of discount bargains. With the family firm of Clarks Shoes behind the venture, it's not surprising to find a shoe museum with regular demonstrations of shoe-making, as well as a picnic area and cafe. But it's not all footwear. Plenty of space has been let to manufacturers of high quality clothing, glassware and pottery.

Discount shopping outlets are familiar in the United States, and more are planned for the UK. They offer a controlled outlet for surplus stock away from town shops; companies with a certain reputation to preserve prefer to dispose of surplus stock in this way than on market stalls. For bargain hunters who are happy to travel fairly far afield, they offer upmarket goods at discount prices.

Cross-Channel trips

For people who live in the south-east, a shopping trip to France is another option. All the cross-Channel ferry operators offer group rates. Most popular for day trips is the shortest route, Dover-Calais, which has the most frequent service. You could take a minibus or you could book seats with one of the many coach companies that offer cross-Channel day trips. From May 1994 you could also go by train, via the Channel Tunnel.

Shopping in Calais's enormous Continental Hypermarket is one of the main attractions. There is also a market in the Place Crevecoeur on Thursday and Saturday mornings, which is especially good for cheese. As time is so limited, it is a good idea for the group organiser to collect as much information as possible beforehand – all the ferry operators will have brochures and leaflets on Calais and other French Channel ports.

Passports are necessary for day trips. Alternatively a British Excursion Document, available to British citizens only, is obtainable from main post offices.

Theatres
London's West End

For group organisers planning a West End theatre visit in London, a telephone call to the Group Sales Box Office (address on p 83) will give you availability and prices of seats for all West End current and forthcoming shows; they will also advise on 'special offers', especially for midweek matinées. They offer a holding service for a limited period to give you time to sell before you confirm – something which an individual theatre probably wouldn't do. They do not charge a booking fee.

The Metropolitan Police Coach Advisory Service for London (address on p 84) will give information on suitable setting down and pick-up points for West End theatre visits.

The Society of West End Theatres' *Disabled Access Guide* lists facilities at every West End theatre, including sound amplification for people with hearing difficulties and wheelchair access. Their monthly *Group Sales Bulletin* gives descriptions of current shows and advance information on future ones.

Regional theatres

Regional theatres are a resource that is often forgotten. As well as the larger theatres in towns and cities, there are also many smaller and fringe theatres outside the London area, often putting on first-class performances.

Regional theatres often offer reductions for party bookings. Group organisers can ask to be put on a priority mailing list to give maximum notice of forthcoming productions. Theatres are often willing to arrange backstage tours.

Concerts

Concerts cover a huge range of musical taste – opera, symphony and chamber concerts, choral works, brass and military bands, swing bands re-creating the Glenn Miller sound of the 1940s, and so on. Regional concert halls host a variety of touring groups. (People who like classical music might also consider going to a BBC audience show – see p 32.)

London's Barbican Centre offers big group discounts for the concert hall. The Barbican is home to the London Symphony Orchestra and the Royal Shakespeare Company. In addition, there is an art gallery and two cinemas. Guided tours are available.

The magazine *Group Travel Organiser* (details on p 89) gives regular London and regional listings for all types of theatrical and musical entertainments.

TV and radio audience shows

Tickets for audience shows are free, and arrangements can usually be made for parties of from 10 to 50 people. Applications should be made at least six weeks in advance, stating the number of tickets required and enclosing a daytime telephone number for the organiser, but there may be a waiting list if a programme is popular. Programmes include classical concerts and comedy shows.

For BBC shows write to BBC Radio and Television Ticket Units at the addresses on page 82. In addition to the London studios, audience shows are also produced in some of the BBC's regional studios.

Applications for tickets for Channel 3 (ITV) audience shows should be made to the regional ITV company that actually makes the programme – many programmes are shown in different ITV regions. If, for example, the programme you are interested in is shown by Anglia, the company for the east of England, but made by Granada, the company for north-west England, it is Granada you need to apply to. Contact the Independent Television Commission Information Office (address on p 84) for the address of the relevant ITV company, or ask in your local library.

Some studios organise guided tours of studio sets and outside locations of famous 'soap' series, for example Granada's *Coronation Street*.

Horse racing

Horse racing is a popular spectator sport, and you don't have to be a racing enthusiast to enjoy a day at the races. Race courses encourage group bookings; contact the club secretary for advance notice of race days.

Many race courses use the indoor stadium facilities at other times for different events – book fairs, antique fairs, etc. Contact the exhibition organiser separately for notice of these events. At Newmarket, there is also the National Horseracing Museum, plus an Equine Tour, which covers the training of modern thoroughbreds and stallions at the studs as well as the race courses.

Other famous sporting venues that offer behind the scenes tours include the Twickenham Rugby Football Union Club and Wembley Stadium. The Wimbledon Lawn Tennis Museum is open throughout the year.

Guided walks

A guided walk can make a good focus for an outing, providing gentle exercise and company, possibly with refreshments at a pub or cafe along the way or at the end.

The leisure departments of many local authorities run programmes of guided walks through local woodlands or countryside. These will be especially appreciated by anyone who enjoys walking but feels reluctant to venture alone across commons and along lonely footpaths. Sometimes there are nature trails.

Guided walks are also popular in towns and cities, particularly where there are history societies. Exploring on foot is the best way to look at old and interesting buildings.

Your local leisure department may be prepared to supply a leader for your party's guided walk. Or you could follow the example of one Age Concern volunteer who enrolled for an adult education 'Discovering London' course expressly so that she would be able to pass on the knowledge she acquired to other group members.

If you are going to guide your party on a country walk yourself, do check out the route a few days beforehand. A gentle, easy spring walk can become a jungle-like trek because of overgrown brambles by the autumn.

For more energetic walks, you could approach the local branch of the Ramblers' Association (address on p 84) for a volunteer guide. Do remind members of your party to wear comfortable and sturdy footwear.

Sporting activities

Local authority leisure and sports centres are increasingly allocating sessions where the over-50s can enjoy swimming, short mat bowling and other sports, often for the first time. Many reluctant participants are greatly encouraged by going to these sessions as one of a group, at least for the first few visits.

Public transport outings

Public transport open trips are popular with certain groups, mainly because of their casual approach and the absence of overt planning.

People do not have to commit themselves in advance, but can make a last-minute decision depending on the weather. People can enjoy as much or as little company as they want, being able to go off on their own once they reach the destination if they wish.

Many retirement fellowship groups of large employers such as the Civil Service and NHS, as well as branches of U3A, run a programme of public transport outings which operate on a 'please-yourself, come-on-the-day' basis. There is usually an announcement about the outing in a newsletter giving the date, the British Rail station plus the train time. People then buy their own tickets on the day, using their Senior Railcards if they have them.

Places like York or Canterbury are typical historic locations which seem to lend themselves to this kind of outing – plenty to see and a manageable size for exploring on foot. Most old county towns have a cathedral or old churches, a museum, a market-place, interesting pubs and cafes as well as pedestrian shopping precincts.

The apparent lack of schedule does not necessarily let the organiser off the hook. An open trip may require some background preparation. The organiser may like to circulate information on places of interest plus entrance fees; suggested eating places with indication of prices, and a sketch map of the chosen location.

Open outings by coach

A variation of the open outing is where transport is by hired coach. This means prior booking, but once at the destination people are free to spend their time as they choose. In areas where public transport is limited, even a short market-day shopping trip (possibly by minibus) to the local town may be appreciated, particularly by people who do not drive themselves or have given up driving.

With any variation on the 'transport only' outing, the advantage of discounted group admission rates to attractions is lost. On the other hand, many party members will qualify for concessionary admission rates as senior citizens, and anyone who has a Senior Railcard will be able to buy train tickets at reduced rates anyway. Some people may also belong to organisations such as the National Trust and English Heritage and so qualify for free or reduced admission to their properties.

Going out for a meal

Dressing up, going out and sharing a sociable lunch with others can make a really enjoyable outing in itself. For suggestions about where to eat and making a booking, see Chapter 7.

Another variation on a sociable shared meal is a 'pot luck' supper, with everyone bringing a shared dish as their contribution. In some areas with people from many different cultures this can give an opportunity to enjoy a wide variety of dishes.

Yet another possibility is a group take-away. Many club premises have somewhere people can eat, and it's often possible to negotiate block orders with a local fish and chip shop or pizza place for either lunches or suppers at a special price.

For suggestions about special occasion meals, such as a Christmas meal or annual reunion, see pages 68–70.

4 General planning

Once you have decided on a venue and a date, it is time to start on the detailed planning and arrangements – basically everything that the group organiser needs to do before the day itself, including:

- working out your planning timetable (ie when different tasks need to be done, and in what order);
- ascertaining numbers, calculating costs, and starting to collect individual contributions (where relevant);
- making detailed plans and timetable for the day, including contingency plans in case the weather is bad or something else goes wrong;
- making provisional bookings and paying deposits;
- finalising numbers and confirming all bookings, by telephone and in writing;
- making sure you have enough helpers for the trip you have chosen and that they all know what is expected of them (see Chapter 5);
- arranging transport and meal stops, and an overnight stay if necessary (see Chapters 6 and 7);
- making sure insurance cover is adequate and other legal requirements are met (see Chapter 8);
- finding out whether any party members have particular medical problems that it would help you to know about;
- making sure everyone concerned is clear about the final arrangements for the day, including pick-up points and time of departure;
- ensuring you have everything you need to hand on the day itself, including a contact sheet, complete with all the phone numbers you might need (see pp 77–78).

Apart from those areas that are covered in other chapters, this chapter looks in turn at these various planning tasks.

A PLANNING MEETING

As suggested on page 11, it is useful to have a meeting at this stage. Alternatively you could make these more detailed decisions at the meeting at which you actually decide where to go. There are various items you might need to discuss and make decisions about, including:

- length of day (provisional departure and arrival home times);
- form of transport (if there is any choice);
- meal stops and other stops en route, bearing in mind the length of your journey (as well as reasonably frequent toilet stops, people may like extra breaks just to stretch their legs);
- eating arrangements at the venue (do people want a pre-arranged meal, or will they make their own arrangements?);
- overnight stop, if there is to be one;
- contingency plans if it rains and your venue is largely an outdoor one.

Checking out the venue

To enable people to make decisions on all these points, you as group organiser will need to have done your homework thoroughly. If you haven't visited the venue yet – perhaps because you didn't have time to visit two or three alternative places – you should go before this meeting if it is at all possible and check out exactly what facilities there are. Things to look out for are toilets, cafes/restaurants/picnic areas, cover in case of wet weather, shops and other attractions.

If some members of your party use wheelchairs, you will need to check the access (see p 19 for an explanation of the English Tourist Board's National Accessible Scheme and for other possible sources of information on access) and see whether there are any special facilities. At some National Trust sites where there are extensive grounds, for example, there are small self-drive battery-powered scooters for hire as well as manual wheelchairs. At other sites, there are golf buggies, taking up to three passengers and driven by volunteers. You will need to check how far away the parking is from the place being visited. A prior visit should also give you a good idea of how many helpers may be needed.

Checking out the journey and possible alternative venues

Check out possible stops for the journey as well. What may look from the outside to be a charming, old-fashioned country pub, ideal for a pleasant drink and toilet stop, may turn out to be crowded, noisy and smoky. Some personal contact beforehand may in any case make all the difference to how your group is received on the day.

Travelling there and back and looking round the venue will also give you a good idea how long the whole outing is likely to take, which will enable you to suggest realistic departure and arrival home times.

As far as transport is concerned, you will need to get estimated journey times and group prices for different forms of transport, where there are alternatives – if you are going to a country venue, your only decision is likely to be how large a coach/minibus you need.

If an overnight stop is planned, you should look into the possibilities, and ideally visit what seem to be the more promising ones.

Finally, if your chosen venue is largely an outdoor one, you will need to give some thought to contingency plans in case it rains. Some prior study of the map plus searching in guide books for possible venues is advisable. If you have time, you may want to visit a couple of possible alternative destinations.

Things you might want to find out from the meeting

There are also various things you might want to find out:

- how many people are planning to come on the day;
- how many people are planning to bring a carer/family member with them – this will give you an indication of how many extra helpers you will need to find;
- confirmation of any special dietary requirements, any requirements or

preferences relating to an overnight stop, and any other requirements (wheelchair access; not too far to walk; toilet on coach, etc).

WORKING OUT YOUR PLANNING TIMETABLE

Once you have held a planning meeting, decisions have been made about the details of the trip, and you know roughly how many people will be coming, you should have a fairly clear idea of what you need to do before the outing. Your next step might be to draw up a planning timetable, which lists everything you still need to do and when you need to do it by.

When working out your schedule you will need to take into account both the size of the outing and your means of communicating with the people who will be going on it. Some large outings will need to be planned very far in advance; some outings can be arranged almost instantly; most will fall somewhere between the two extremes. Group visits should always be arranged in advance, even for a small group. The organiser should telephone to make sure the group's visit isn't going to clash with that of another party.

The annual outing

A large-scale event laid on by a company for retired employees who are scattered around the country and will be converging on the venue from different starting points will probably involve planning at least a year ahead. Any popular venue such as a commercially run stately home which can be hired for private exclusive use for the day will need at least this much notice for an advance booking. Arrangements are usually on a grand scale for this kind of outing. You could be talking about numbers of around 600. 'It's only 12 coaches,' commented one organiser accustomed to this kind of mega outing.

If you are just responsible for organising a coach from a particular area, on the other hand, you will obviously not need to plan so far ahead. People are usually kept informed about such events through a regular newsletter, so your preparation run-up will depend very much on how frequent that is.

The instant outing

At the opposite end of the spectrum, a pensioners' club that meets weekly, with access to its own minibus and driver, can make an almost instant decision to go out and make the most of the afternoon sunshine at a local park or countryside beauty spot.

NUMBERS, COSTINGS AND CONTRIBUTIONS

Checking on numbers for the outing

However much you would like to be flexible, it is almost impossible for a group organiser to get on with planning a trip if you don't have a fair idea how many people are going on it. You won't know how large a restaurant you need for a meal stop, how big a hotel you need for an overnight stop, how big a coach you need. As far as the coach is concerned, this will affect your costings too, since a large coach is likely to work out considerably cheaper per head than a small coach or minibus.

Although there will always be some people with genuine reasons why they cannot make a firm decision yet, any organiser will have to be firm about the need for people to commit themselves to coming on the outing at an early stage (at the detailed planning meeting, if there is one). Ideally you should start collecting contributions straightaway. If places are likely to be short, this will obviously not be difficult.

There may well be a need for a waiting list for popular trips or for visits where numbers are restricted. A party tour of the House of Commons, for example, is limited to 16 (and is arranged by contacting your local MP).

If you want to try out a new idea for a trip but aren't sure how popular it will be, a minibus outing is a good way to test people's response.

Group organiser 'We tried out a mystery drive into the country with a pub lunch thrown in and soon found ourselves with a waiting list.'

Calculating the cost

When working out the cost of a trip, it is wise to round up to the nearest 50p or pound. It is always better to err on the side of slightly overestimating the full amount rather than having to ask for an additional sum at a later stage. Any money that is left over can be used to pay for extra teas/coffees if you have an extra stop on the way home, or it can go into a communal kitty towards future outings, or possibly towards a refund for anyone who is ill and unable to make it on the day.

Costings checklist – what to include

Transport – usually coach hire. The amount per head will depend on how large the coach is and whether it is full. It is a good idea to include a tip for the driver in the seat price.

Entrance fee to tourist attraction (including any concessions for groups, senior citizens or helpers).

Pre-booked meals, either at the attraction or on the way.

Refreshments at scheduled stops.

Administrative expenses – stamps, phone calls, faxes, etc (these may be covered by your organisation).

Bear in mind that the numbers for coach seats and entrance fees might not tally if helpers are involved, as helpers may be admitted to attractions free (see p 56). In this case you may need (or already have) a policy concerning helpers and their financial contributions. Do you charge them only for the travel and meal elements, or do you spread the costs overall and charge everyone the same?

Example

This is a costing for a trip from Beckenham, Kent, to Leonardslee Gardens, Nr Horsham, East Sussex, some 2–2½ hours drive away.

Provisional figures

These were based on an estimated break-even take-up of 40 places, a first-time guess on the part of the organiser.

Group admission rate from May,

azalea time £3 × 40	£120
Basic 53-seater coach	£180
Tip for driver	£20
	£320

This worked out at a cost of £8 per person (£320 ÷ 40).

Revised figures

The 53 coach seats were quickly taken up. In view of the good response, the committee decided that the organiser needn't pay.

Group admission £3 × 53	£159
Coach	£180
Tip for driver	£15
Coffee and biscuits at a pub on the way £1 × 54 (53 plus driver)	£54
Administrative phone calls	£5
Total cost	**£413**
Total income (52 × £8)	**£416**

The tip for the driver was reduced following a conversation with another local group organiser, who felt the original £20 was over-generous. The coffee quote was an exceptionally cheap one from a pub in the *Yellow Pages*. Some places had quoted as much as £2.50 per head.

As a result of the better than estimated take-up of places, the organiser was thus able to include the cost of refreshments in the original price. The profit of £3 the organiser spent on a tin of boiled sweets to offer to people as they boarded the coach. This has now become a recognised trademark of this organiser's outings.

Paying for the trip

The following are some of the different ways in which an outing may be paid for:

■ Party members contribute the full cost to the nearest rounded-up amount. In this case you will need to collect deposits as soon as possible, and to set an absolute deadline for payment of the full amount. Otherwise you may find yourself having to pay in advance for a trip which party members have not fully committed themselves to.

- There may be an ongoing fundraising programme of bring-and-buy sales, jumble sales, raffles, coffee mornings, bingo, etc, all of which are social events in themselves.

- Members of a club may make regular weekly contributions to an outings fund, an arrangement which many pensioners' clubs prefer, rather than expecting members to pay out a largish sum all in one go. Anyone who is ill or who doesn't go on a trip will get a refund of their contributions, or they will be carried forward.

- A special outing – perhaps a visit to a Christmas show – may be funded or partially funded by a sponsor, such as a local Rotary Club or a neighbourhood pub. One way the organiser can show people's appreciation for this kind of generosity is to send a news item, preferably with photographs, to the local paper.

- A company or organisation may foot part of the bill for a retired staff outing. But even when the firm's subsidy is a large one, organisers stress the importance of a reasonable contribution from party members. If the event doesn't cost them anything, people can be very cavalier about turning up on the day, and this can cause havoc with the organiser's arrangements.

No organiser would plan a trip that was beyond the means of most prospective party members, but there may easily be one or two people who would like to come on an outing but really can't afford it. Where there is an outings fund, raised either through fundraising events or through regular contributions, or where a sponsor or company is footing all or part of the bill, this shouldn't raise any problems. It is only where people are paying the full cost of the trip individually that you would have to make any special arrangements.

There are many attractions with free admission, especially museums. You'll find them listed in tourist guides, and it's a good idea to compile your own list for when funds are low.

MAKING DETAILED PLANS AND A TIMETABLE FOR THE DAY

Timetable for the day

If you have visited the venue yourself and made the journey there and back, and decisions have been made about all the details of the day – meal stops, frequency of other stops on the way, a possible extra short stop at a local beauty spot on the way back, and so on – you should be in a position to work out an exact timetable for the day: when you will arrive for your lunch stop, how long you will need for lunch, when you will arrive at your main destination, when you will leave, when you will get home. You will then be in a position to make bookings, as discussed on pages 48–49. (See also Chapters 6 and 7 on booking transport, meals and overnight stops.)

If you haven't been able to do a dummy run yourself, you will have to rely on looking at maps, consulting the coach company, and talking to someone at the venue about how long it usually takes to look at everything.

When working this out, you will obviously need to allow more time for each stage than it took you. It will take longer for 50 people to get in and out of a coach than it took you to get in and out of your car, especially if any members of your party use wheelchairs. If you are a party of any size, you will create your own queues in toilets, at tills in shops, in cafes and so on. In addition, you may have to wait for people to turn up at the coach pick-up point – how long you are prepared to wait is something else you will have to decide, and you will then have to make sure everyone is absolutely clear about the position.

When you have worked all this out, you may find you have to revise the provisional time for arriving home that you arranged at your planning meeting.

Meal arrangements

Meal arrangements should have been discussed fully at your planning meeting. If there is to be a meal stop en route or a pre-arranged meal at the venue, the group organiser will need to arrange this in advance, as discussed in Chapter 7. In any case, the organiser will need to know whether or not to include the price of a meal in the total cost of the outing.

If people have decided to make their own arrangements, either bringing their own food, buying a take-away on the spot, or using local facilities like pubs and cafes on an individual basis, the organiser won't have any arrangements to make.

Contingency plans in case of bad weather

If the outing your group has decided on is mainly outdoors, you should have discussed the possibility of bad weather and the need for an alternative indoor attraction. Every organiser needs a Plan B just in case the weather is truly awful and shows no signs of clearing up.

You might want to consider a last-minute switch to a nearby alternative destination. You could, for example, substitute Margate for Broadstairs because there is more to do indoors in Margate. A Scarborough expedition could easily be diverted to York. 'York's wonderful for a wet day,' commented one organiser whose group found refuge in the railway museum there. If the coach has a mobile phone or paging system, it may be possible for the driver to check on weather conditions a few miles away.

Alternatively, you could cut down the length of time to be spent at the agreed venue and instead take in an extra stop somewhere else along the way. An indoor shopping centre (see p 29) could come into its own here – provided everyone in your party likes shopping.

Group organiser 'If it's too wet and windy at Whitley Bay – and I've never known it not wet and windy there – you're near enough to the MetroCentre at Gateshead.'

The possibility of switching destination is worth mentioning to the coach company when booking, because it's important that the driver should know the way to the alternative venue, and that the coach company should be happy with the arrangement.

Contingency plans in case things go wrong

- What do you do if someone doesn't turn up for the coach? How long do you wait?

- What do you do if a member of your party has an accident or is taken ill?

- What do you do if someone gets soaked to the skin in an unexpected shower/collapses with heat stroke?

These are just a few of the things which can go wrong on an outing. No group organiser can foresee all the possibilities and take precautions against them – you would never get your party to the destination at all. On the other hand, there are certain basic precautions that are worth considering.

In case people fail to turn up at the initial pick-up point:

- You can ask people to arrive early enough for you to make a last-minute phone call if someone doesn't turn up. Make sure the pick-up point is in reach of a phone, and that there is somewhere to shelter in case of rain. And make sure you have the phone numbers of all your group.

- You should make sure everyone knows your phone number or another contact number where they can ring in case of illness or other emergency on the day.

- You will need to decide how long you are prepared to wait for latecomers, and to make sure everyone is clear about the situation. This also applies to pick-ups after stops en route and at the venue itself.

The question of what to do if someone has an accident or becomes ill raises the more general issues of whether to take a car with you on the day and whether to have a deputy organiser.

Do you take a car?

An extra car can be useful on an outing:

- as a link, especially if there is more than one pick-up point;

- to pick up stragglers and/or latecomers;

- to take someone who has been injured or taken seriously ill to the Accident and Emergency Department of a local hospital;

- to take someone home who has become ill and is unable to carry on for the rest of the day.

If the organiser travels in their own car, this does separate them from the rest of the party, but the extra car doesn't have to be the organiser's; it could belong to a helper – or the deputy organiser.

If the driver is not the owner of the vehicle – if, for example, you hand over the keys of your car to a helper so that you can stay with the main party – you must make sure the insurance covers the car being driven by people other than the named driver(s).

Accident and Emergency Departments nowadays usually give some indication of how long the waiting time is likely to be, according to the severity of the injury. If there is a long wait and the injury is minor, you could consider giving on-the-spot first aid and going to a hospital nearer home.

Do you have a deputy organiser?

The issue of whether to have a fully briefed deputy organiser is discussed more fully on pages 9–10. Where the organiser decides to bring a car on the outing, it makes particularly good sense to have a deputy who can drive the car too – either to remain with the party if you go off on an emergency trip or to deal with the emergency.

Whether or not you have a deputy organiser, it is vital to have your schedule/itinerary clearly documented. If someone else does have to take over from you, they can then be given a file containing details of the day, booking/payment receipts, contact numbers, etc.

If you decide not to have a deputy organiser, it is a useful mental exercise to consider who you would ask for help in an emergency, particularly if you had to hand over the party to someone else.

Having talked through the various potential disasters, it will seem like a positive achievement in itself if you don't need to activate any of your contingency arrangements on the day.

MAKING BOOKINGS

You will obviously need to have made certain enquiries about costs, group rates, payment terms, etc, at a much earlier stage, before you even made a definite proposal for a venue to your prospective party members, as suggested on page 22. Now that you are in a position to go ahead and make bookings, you will need to confirm with the attraction:

- cost of admission and group rates;

- how many people are needed to qualify for group rates (this could be 15 or 20 or 30; it will vary from place to place);

- whether they have any concessions for senior citizens, if group rates aren't applicable because your group isn't big enough;

- whether they have any concessions for helpers – some attractions let helpers in free, as explained on page 56;

- how much deposit you need to pay – this could be 10 per cent, but again varies from place to place;

- when you will need to pay the balance;

- whether they accept credit card payment – paying by credit card is obviously convenient for the organiser, as it means you can book over the phone (you may need to increase your credit limit);

- whether they offer any discounts for prompt payment or for not paying by credit card;

- whether you still have to pay the full amount if some members of your party are unable to come on the day. This may be something you will haggle over on the day rather than sort out in advance.

Group bookings always need to be made in advance – the larger your party, the further ahead you will probably need to book. If the place you are visiting is fairly small, they may not be able to cope with more than one large party at the same time.

It is common sense not to pay the balance before you need to. Apart from anything else, if you find that your group consists of less people than you originally booked for, it always seems easier to avoid paying for people who are not there than to get a refund of money you have already paid.

Whether you have to pay for people who cannot come may depend partly on the size of the attraction. If it is a large place, it will make little difference whether your party consists of 20 or 25 people, and it is unlikely that any special arrangements will have been made to accommodate you. If the place is very small, booking for 25 may mean more or less booking it exclusively, and will certainly rule out other groups being there at the same time, so they are more likely to insist that you pay for the full number of people.

Similar enquiries will need to be made when you are booking transport, meals and accommodation, as discussed in Chapters 6 and 7.

FINDING OUT ABOUT PEOPLE'S MEDICAL CONDITIONS

Particularly where a regular programme of outings is concerned, some group organisers may feel they would like information about certain medical conditions people may have, such as diabetes or epilepsy, in case emergency treatment is necessary. Opinions are divided about whether asking for such information is an intrusion on people's privacy.

People could be asked to fill in a confidential questionnaire about their health and any medication they are taking, as they probably would be prior to going on a group holiday. It should be made clear that the information will be regarded as confidential, and this point should be stressed with helpers.

It is always a good idea to check whether there are first aid facilities at the venue itself, and where the nearest hospital with an Accident and Emergency Department is, as well as taking a first aid kit with you.

First aid tip

Any organiser or helper who passed a first aid exam a few years ago should buy a newly updated copy of the St John Ambulance *First Aid Manual* or the British Red Cross *Practical First Aid* (details on pp 88 and 90) or preferably attend a refresher course. Guidelines for basic resuscitation have been altered in order to standardise recommendations throughout Europe. The main change relates to the recovery position for people who are unconscious.

LETTING PEOPLE KNOW THE FINAL ARRANGEMENTS

You could confirm the final arrangements for the day at a meeting or through a newsletter or special mailing. Even if you do it at a meeting, it is wise to put all the details in writing as well. You will need to let people know the following:

- pick-up places and times for the coach at the beginning and end of the trip – a sketch map could be useful, particularly for the pick-up place at the venue;

- how long you are prepared to wait for people who do not turn up for the coach on time;

- your telephone number in case of last-minute problems;

- any special clothing they will need for the trip, such as strong, comfortable shoes for walking;

- anything else people might need (eg passports and foreign currency for a cross-Channel trip);

- approximate return time for anyone being met by car.

5 Helpers

It is not always necessary to have extra helpers on an outing. Whether you need extra helpers and how many you need will depend on who is going on the outing and where you are going. If all the members of the party are fit and active, there will obviously be no need for helpers. If most people in the party are fairly fit but a few are a bit unsteady on their feet, there may well be no need for support beyond the fitter members of the party offering the less fit an occasional steadying arm to lean on or assistance with getting up and down steps.

It is only where there are a good many frail or disabled people in the party, particularly if they use wheelchairs, that you are likely to need extra helpers. The more walking and the more going up and down steps the outing involves, the more helpers will be needed. Never assume that other members of the party will want to spend the whole day pushing a wheelchair, even if they are fit enough to do so.

FINDING EXTRA HELPERS

Where extra help is needed, beyond what would be provided on an informal basis by the fitter members of the party, this is likely to come either from family carers or relatives or from among the group's regular volunteers.

Family carers or relatives

Where they are available, family carers or relatives are an ideal source of extra help.

Age Concern group organiser 'We deliberately plan our outings on Saturdays and Sundays so that younger relatives, who are reliable and familiar escorts, are available. It's also worth noting that an elderly carer is often as much in need of a day out as the person they are caring for, who may be attending a club or day centre.'

In addition to helping, an invited companion can provide reassurance for a group member who is anxious about being a nuisance or a worry to others. Sometimes a fall or minor mishap on a previous outing may put someone off going on a subsequent outing, and the thought of being able to bring someone with them can make all the difference.

Regular volunteers

Many groups will have existing volunteers who probably take part in all sorts of activities other than helping on outings. Where they are going to act as helpers, it is important not to stretch their physical capabilities too far, as the chief officer of a voluntary organisation explained:

Chief officer 'Anna, in her late fifties, was a hard-working and willing helper both in the charity shop and in the pop-in parlour. She had no hesitation in agreeing to help on an outing until she found herself pushing a 17-stone elderly man in a wheelchair around Kew Gardens for an entire afternoon. She put on a brave face at the time, but suffered at home for quite a few days afterwards with a strained back. Much to her credit, Anna remained a loyal and willing helper; but she could so easily have given up altogether.'

BRIEFING HELPERS

It is vital for the group organiser to make sure that helpers are kept fully informed of all the details of arrangements and also of any last-minute changes, particularly on a long day out.

Helpers need to be familiar with arrangements for toilet stops, meals, return time, etc, in order to be able to answer any questions they may be asked. Some people are great worriers, and some may be confused; being told exactly what is happening can be very reassuring. Someone who is feeling anxious about feeling travel sick or needing the toilet, for example, may be more likely to confide in a helper than to trouble the organiser.

Where there are disabled people in the party, it is important to give helpers specific tasks when loading and unloading coaches, for example:

- helpers to load/unload wheelchairs;
- helpers to be/remain on the coach;
- helpers to be in a position to load/unload the hoist.

This avoids confusion on the day, as helpers will be able to take up their allotted positions without further discussion. Another important task for helpers is to make sure that belongings are not left behind at stopping places or on the coach at the end of the day.

There may be people who need to have a specially alert eye kept on them because of a medical condition such as diabetes or epilepsy. They may need to take tablets during the day, something which could easily be forgotten with the excitement and change of routine. Helpers should be told of cases like this, but discreetly so as not to cause embarrassment to the people concerned.

If any party members need a special diet, a helper should be made responsible for making sure their needs are met.

Helpers need to know what is expected of them, but if they feel it is all hard work and no fun they may not want to help on an outing again. It is therefore up to the organiser to make sure the helpers don't feel overburdened and to try to make the day an enjoyable one for them too.

This is vital for other members of the party as well. If the helpers look miserable, this will tend to communicate itself to other people. If they look as if they are having a good time, this will help make the outing more enjoyable for everyone.

Checklist of items on which helpers should be briefed

- Coach details: pick-up points, start and return times.
- Details of the schedule: toilet stops, meal arrangements, time of arrival at attraction, etc.
- Tasks when loading and unloading the coach.
- Special tasks for the rest of the outing, for example pushing a particular person's wheelchair.
- Degree of mobility of different members of the party and the amount of help they require.
- Anyone who has particular health problems, or who needs medication during the day or a special diet.
- Location of the first aid box.

TRAINING HELPERS

The group organiser will need to find out whether volunteers have had any kind of training in first aid (see p 49), assisting wheelchair users, passenger assistance techniques or 'disability awareness'. Organisers may also welcome the opportunity to attend short familiarisation sessions themselves, particularly if they are involved with frail or disabled people.

If the organiser is working under the umbrella of a larger organisation, it may be possible to discuss issues such as volunteer selection and training needs at greater length with the umbrella organisation.

Wheelchair training

Where pushing manual wheelchairs is concerned, not only should volunteers be reasonably strong and fit, but they also need some basic familiarisation with handling wheelchairs if the comfort and safety of users are to be ensured.

The manoeuvres which put people in wheelchairs most at risk are going up and down steps and kerbs. Never rely on the brakes of a wheelchair. They wear out easily and are often out of alignment.

Passenger assistance training

If the outing involves travelling by coach or minibus, you may want to arrange a passenger assistance training session for volunteers. If your organisation has its own minibus, you can use that, parked safely off the road. Ideally you need a willing wheelchair user/volunteer as guinea pig. All escorts and helpers should understand the following procedures:

- how to use wheelchair clamps or straps;
- how to use passenger restraints;
- how to operate lifts, ramps and doors.

Disability awareness training

Briefly, disability awareness is a matter of being sensitive to other people's needs, of treating others as you'd like to be treated yourself. Here are a few golden rules:

- Be patient and allow people to move at their own pace, however slow.
- Don't pull or grab hold of people who are unsteady or slow. Offer a supporting arm to lean on or a steadying hand down steps.
- When people have a visual disability, don't creep up on them. Make your presence known by telling them your name and who you are. Ask whether they need help.
- When people have a hearing disability, speak clearly and slowly, and face them, as they may be able to lipread.
- Be patient with those who have speech difficulties. Listen carefully and do not assume they are unintelligible. Offer a pen and paper if necessary.

Where to go for information and training

The Community Transport Association (address on p 83) produces a range of publications including the *Community Transport Manual on Driver Assessment and Training*. This has detailed sections on assisting wheelchair users, passenger assistance techniques and disability awareness.

Training sessions for helpers are not widely available and will usually have to be paid for. The Community Transport Association runs courses for helpers, both nationally and on a regional basis; it might also be able to offer advice about other sources of training. You could also try contacting your local social services department for advice.

CONCESSIONS

Admission fees for helpers and escorts for disabled or older people are often waived at visitor attractions. This concession might not necessarily be mentioned in guide books or publicity material, so the group organiser should always ask when making preliminary enquiries. According to Disabled Living, a Manchester-based charity specialising in day trips (address on p 83), price strategy varies from place to place as well as from year to year.

Disabled Living worker 'I never realised how much you can haggle over discounts and letting helpers in for free. You have to play it by ear – either being cheeky or putting on the charm.'

If the outing is to take place on a weekday when there are fewer visitors, any such request will naturally be more favourably received. Most National Trust properties allow helpers for disabled people in free of charge, but this must be by prior arrangement with the specific property concerned.

6 Transport

Although there are outings for which rail will be the obvious choice, for the majority of outings you will probably want to use a coach or minibus – possibly a specially adapted one if several members of your party are disabled. Some groups that go on regular outings may have their own minibus, or even a coach.

This chapter looks in some detail at choosing a coach company and hiring a coach, making sure that the coach you get meets all your requirements and that you get the best possible terms. It also looks at minibuses and specially adapted transport, and discusses the circumstances in which rail might be the most convenient form of transport.

HIRING A COACH

Choosing a coach company

Many people who plan outings, especially those who arrange only occasional outings, tend to work on the 'devil you know' principle and stick to the company they have used in the past. But it can pay to shop around, as demonstrated by Age Concern Somerset, a county organisation with many groups affiliated to their 'Time Out' club.

A year or so ago they planned a series of outings and asked local coach companies for quotes. By going out to tender this way, the Time Out club can now offer trips at very competitive rates.

Group organiser 'We chose the cheapest and haven't regretted it. Other firms who also tendered approached us subsequently and offered to lower their prices.'

This is a good example of how a large umbrella organisation with sufficient buying power can greatly assist smaller clubs in the area. Not only has this arrangement saved money, it has also cut down on the time that individual organisers used to spend getting quotes. It has also saved them having to put money upfront as deposits in the early stages of planning an outing.

But being cheap and reliable is only part of the equation. Organisers should also ask themselves:

- Are the coaches sufficiently comfortable?
- Do they have all the facilities you require, for example a toilet on board?
- Are the drivers friendly and do they always know the best routes?
- Are the payment terms convenient?

When comparing quotations from different firms, always bear in mind that you can only compare like with like. Extras might include a toilet, microphone and PA system, drinks, vending machine, or video. Always make sure exactly what you are getting for your money.

If you have time, it is a good idea to ask if you can come and see the range of vehicles available. If you are not sure how many people will be going on an outing, it is wise to choose a coach company that has a range of vehicle sizes.

Ask about payment terms as well. It is common practice to pay a deposit before the trip. Ask how much this is, when it has to be paid, and when the balance is due.

Remember that coach hire is likely to be more expensive at weekends than on weekdays.

Checking on reliability

Ways to find a reliable coach firm include:

- asking for a personal recommendation from another group organiser;
- ringing Crusader Group Travel (the party booking agency for National

Express – address on p 83) for the name of their associated coach
company in your area;

■ looking in the *Yellow Pages* or the *Thomson Directory* for associate
members of the Bus and Coach Council.

One-off trip or a regular contract?

You may find you are offered better terms if you are planning a regular
programme of outings than if you only want it for a one-off trip. If you are
planning regular outings, you should let the firm know that you are interested in a regular contract if the terms are right. Also let them know you
are seeking other quotes.

Many coach companies greatly appreciate their regular customers. One
group organiser in Kent is offered a regular yearly free trip to London for
her group to see the Regent Street Christmas lights as a token of the
firm's appreciation of the business she brings them all year round.

Checking your requirements
Numbers

Every organiser is juggling with two sets of numbers, provisional and
final. However, provided you choose a company with a wide enough
range of vehicle sizes, 'having to fill the coach' shouldn't be a problem.

Sometimes a coach company, acting in the capacity of tour operator, may
offer your party a number of seats on a shared outing basis. Much
depends on who the other group passengers are and how compatible they
might be with your party. This arrangement can be risky. If you are going
to share an outing, you may prefer to pick your own companion group.

Much the same consideration applies to block-booking seats for your
party on a pre-packaged commercial coach tour.

Wheelchairs

With most coaches you can take out a couple of seats if necessary to
make space for wheelchairs. Hoist facilities are a good idea.

Toilet on board

Preferences vary here. You might like to consult your members. Some organisers say they would not travel without a toilet on board. On the other hand, if you plan to have frequent stops anyway so that people can stretch their legs, it may not be necessary.

Mobile phone

A phone on the coach could be useful in case emergency services are needed by any member of the party.

Your group's requirements obviously cannot be looked at in isolation. How long the journey takes and whether or not there are service stations en route will also be relevant. The longer the travelling time, the more comforts you may need.

Checklist for hiring a coach

- Get a rough idea of numbers in the party.
- Depending on journey distance, work out your requirements: toilet on board; number of pick-up and set-down points you need; number of breaks (unscheduled breaks and detours may be charged as extras). Do you prefer a more leisurely scenic drive or a fast dash on the motorway?
- Ring round coach companies to discuss your requirements and ask for quotes.
- Compare prices and terms – and their attitude towards customers.
- Decide on a company and make a provisional booking.
- Confirm booking.

The role of the driver

The contribution made by the driver to the success of an outing should not be underestimated. Drivers play a supporting role but it is a key one. Coach companies certainly realise this; in fact, in their publicity material they often make great play of having 'nice friendly drivers'.

If you like your driver, make sure you find out his or her name. Then you can request that driver again the next time. Coach companies encourage this kind of feedback.

Tipping the driver is one way of saying thank you. A less embarrassing way to do this than passing round the hat is for the organiser to take care of this on behalf of the rest of the party and to allow for it in the total cost of the outing.

Smoking

National Express, Britain's major national coach network, has now banned smoking on the grounds that nine out of ten passengers, even smokers, prefer smoke-free travel. It's always preferable to warn people in advance of a non-smoking policy, and you can promise regular breaks along the way.

Hiring a coach from a voluntary organisation

You might be able to hire a coach from a voluntary organisation if there is one in your area that owns its own coach. Age Concern Coventry, for example, owns a 30-seater coach with removable seats that allow for two wheelchairs plus a tail-lift. The coach is available on a day-hire basis within a 50-mile radius to any of a number of affiliated pensioner clubs in the area. This facility is so popular that by the first week in January, the coach is invariably booked every day for the rest of the year.

MINIBUSES

You can hire a minibus plus driver just as you can a coach. Your company or organisation may also have its own minibus, with or without a driver.

Should one of your members offer to drive the minibus, you will need to check whether the insurance specifies any upper age limits for drivers. If it does, it may be possible to shop around and find a different company. No special public service vehicle (PSV) licence is required to drive a vehicle carrying between 8 and 17 passengers, but this may change in the near future.

Practice for the driver

For the sake of the general comfort and safety of your passengers, you also need to be sure that any potential driver who has not driven a minibus before is willing to put in some practice driving before the trip. Experienced car drivers who have never driven a large vehicle can need up to four hours' training, preferably accompanied by an experienced minibus driver.

A minibus should be seen as a small bus and not a large car. For example, a car driver may not be sufficiently aware of the correct use of wing mirrors, a technique used more with bus and truck driving. Well over half of all minibus insurance claims are the fault of the driver, and are preventable. Many happen when the driver is manoeuvring or reversing; on a day's outing, parking is going to be almost as crucial as the actual driving.

SPECIALISED TRANSPORT

Mobility coaches or welfare minibuses for disabled people can be hired privately from companies which specialise in supplying adapted vehicles with side and/or tail lifts, clamping for wheelchairs, etc.

They may also supply a driver who is used to assisting elderly and disabled people, and possibly also escorts, although most organisers will want to bring their own volunteers. If you are using this kind of service, do make sure you provide the company with accurate information about party members, for example how many can get out of their wheelchairs. A frequent complaint is that group organisers often do not know sufficient details about people's mobility problems.

You can find mobility coach and welfare minibus firms by:

- looking in the *Yellow Pages* or the *Thomson Directory*;
- asking local organisations run by or for disabled people;
- asking your local social services department (many firms are under contract to supply welfare transport to the local authority).

Other sources

It may also be possible to beg, borrow or hire specialised transport from:

- a local organisation which is a member of the Community Transport Association (address on p 83);
- a local Age Concern group which has specialised transport of its own;
- a local authority social services department which has its own welfare fleet vehicles;
- a voluntary organisation for disabled people.

In all cases you will want to ensure that the person doing the driving is properly trained and that helpers are familiar with the passenger assistance techniques outlined on page 55.

GOING BY RAIL

There are many destinations where rail is the obvious choice, at least for the fit and active. Going by train is convenient when you are going somewhere where there might be a lot of traffic or difficulties parking, as in most city centres. Special trains are often laid on for race meetings where there is a convenient local station. There are particularly good services between London and many of the south-east coastal resorts, which are on commuter lines.

With the privatisation of British Rail on the cards, anything could change. Meantime, try your regional Telephone Enquiry Bureau and ask about their arrangements for group travel. Network SouthEast has a Promotions Manager for Group Travel Enquiries whom you can ask for up-to-date leaflets, including special discount trips.

Group rates and other concessions

If you are travelling in a group by rail, you need only ten fare-paying passengers travelling to the same destination to qualify for a 25 per cent group reduction. However, individuals will not qualify for Senior Railcard concessions as well, so this is particularly useful if people in your group do not have Senior Railcards.

Seat reservations for parties are free, but you will need to book early.

On open outings, where individuals travel on a certain train bound for an agreed destination (see pp 33–34), members can use their individual Senior Railcards, offering a third off most leisure fares. Gift vouchers (£16) are now available for the purchase of these. The Government has promised that Senior Railcards will continue after privatisation.

Rail travel is not to be recommended for a group of disabled people.

TRAVEL FOR DISABLED PEOPLE

A charitable organisation called Tripscope (address on p 87) can offer advice and information on how to plan every step of any journey within the scope and limitations of an older and/or disabled individual. This might involve a local dial-a-ride or Taxicard scheme, plus British Rail or London Underground, avoiding stations with crowded escalators. Tripscope has access to nationwide specialist travel information and can save a busy organiser hours of time.

ATS Travel Ltd and Can Be Done Ltd (addresses on p 82) both specialise in arranging holidays for disabled people, both for groups and for individuals, but they will also provide travel advice and arrange day outings.

7 Eating out and overnight stops

Attitudes and appetites vary enormously, as do budgets. Sometimes people resent paying what they consider to be greatly over the odds for meals and snacks on a day out; they much prefer to bring their own food and a thermos flask. For others, enjoying a meal cooked by someone else is a welcome change and all part of the pleasure of the day.

These differing views make for complications and emphasise the need for some degree of prior consensus. The organiser needs to investigate all the possible alternatives available. Vegetarians and anyone on a special diet should be reminded to inform the organiser in good time beforehand.

This chapter looks at various options for meals on a day out. It also covers going out for a special occasion meal, such as a reunion, and arranging an overnight stop.

MEALS ON A DAY OUT

Meals at the venue

Your chosen visitor attraction may offer catering facilities, but the group organiser needs to find out what the knife and fork symbol really means. What sort of food is on offer? Do they do party bookings? Is it self-service or waitress service?

If you want to make a group booking, this will have to be done in advance; timing may be critical if other parties are visiting on the same day. If service is to be reasonably speedy and efficient, the menu may need to be agreed beforehand. With pre-booked meals the cost of the meal will probably be included in the overall cost of the outing, with the organiser paying the bill on behalf of the rest of the party. The obvious disadvantage of a pre-booked meal is that you are tied to being at a certain place at a predetermined time.

If people decide not to eat as a group but to make their own arrangements and eat as and when they like, then they will pay for their own meals if they eat in a cafe or restaurant. It is worth thinking about numbers here. If there is only one restaurant at the venue and you are a large party, this may mean queuing for a considerable time.

If some people prefer to bring their own food and have a picnic, the organiser will need to check out picnic areas in advance – what about shelter if it is rainy? – plus the availability of hot drinks.

If the outing is an 'open' one (see pp 33–34) and people are making their own meal arrangements, a sketch map giving the location of any known eating places can be useful, particularly to anyone who hasn't been there before.

Meal stops en route

If you want a meal stop on the way, it is always a good idea to book in advance and agree the menu so as to avoid undue delays.

Should you, for any reason, stop unexpectedly for refreshments other than at a motorway service station – say in a small pub – it may be advisable for the organiser to go in ahead and check with the manager that they can cope with a party of your size.

Group organiser 'Publicans have a reputation for not liking parties who don't spend a lot on drinks, so I went ahead and asked if it was OK first. He was marvellous. He got out tables and chairs and even rustled up a piano player for a sing-song.'

Different places you can eat
Pubs

Pub lunches are usually good value for money, provided there is sufficient space for your party. Many pubs can offer a private dining room for a pre-booked party, while individual members can buy their own drinks at the bar.

Small family-owned restaurants

Small family-owned restaurants often provide a friendly atmosphere for any kind of not too formal meal, as long as numbers are within reason. While the advertised menu will give a rough indication of range and price, it may be easier for a group booking if individuals choose from a more limited pre-selection of dishes. This kind of arrangement places less stress on a small kitchen and makes for speedier service. A personal visit to discuss arrangements with the manager beforehand should ensure a warm welcome for your party.

A group visit can offer an ideal opportunity to explore eating out in different types of restaurant. The City of Bradford, for example, with over 70 authentic Asian restaurants, publishes a 'Flavours of Asia' leaflet, with hints on finding your way around the menu plus descriptions of regional dishes.

The Mature Choice scheme

Not everyone wants a large meal at lunchtime, particularly older people who may have small appetites anyway. Mature Choice is a scheme from the Guild of Master Caterers designed to promote 'a comfortable meal at a comfortable price'. Around 1,500 pubs, restaurants and hotels associated with the Guild offer Mature Choice, which means an ordinary meal reduced in both size and price but not in quality. Look out for the Mature Choice logo. You can contact the head office of the Guild of Master Caterers (address on p 84) for a list of local participating members.

The big chains

The big chains are very much looking for this kind of business and will often agree a special menu. The main advantage of a chain is that menus and service are standardised. Having sampled one restaurant, you know what to expect in the others. If you find one that suits your party, you can ask for a leaflet giving details of others further afield.

In London

Garfunkels, with 20 restaurants located in central London, have recently launched a party booking scheme with a choice of three set menus. The Spaghetti House Group have private rooms for parties in some of their restaurants. For group bookings for 15 to 150 people, contact the marketing manager. Pizza Express have over 50 restaurants in London and the south; they also have some private rooms available.

Outside London

Outside London, look out for countrywide chains such as Brewer's Fayre, Wayside Inns, Chef & Brewer, Beefeater, Wheelers and Harvester, many of which will already be familiar names to your members.

Harry Ramsdens is a specialist fish and chip chain, with its own Senior Citizens menu. Restaurants are located in Castlefield, Manchester; the Promenade, Blackpool; Guiseley, Yorkshire; and more recently in Birmingham, Bristol and Heathrow Airport.

Checklist for arranging meals on a day out

- Check out facilities and prices at the location itself.
- Check if there are more attractive or better value for money alternatives nearby. Would a meal stop fit in with the journey timetable?
- Find out party members' preferences and make a decision.
- If you are making a group booking, ask for a menu.
- Agree menu with party members. Any vegetarians or special diets?
- Make a provisional booking.
- Confirm booking nearer the time.

SPECIAL OCCASION MEALS

Sometimes an outing may simply consist of going out for a meal, rather than the meal being part of a day out, as suggested on page 35. Outings like this can take place at any time but they are often arranged for a special occasion.

A Christmas meal

The most popular time for a celebratory meal is without doubt Christmas, when you may find yourselves competing for bookings with every office party in town. Sometimes when a pub or restaurant has developed a particularly good reputation, you need to book months in advance. In other words, you may have to start thinking about your Christmas lunch way back in August. Often when a group has discovered an especially good venue, they book from one Christmas to the next.

One solution might be to consider shifting the meal from Christmas to the New Year – not New Year's Eve, which will probably be just as busy, but early January. An event for people to look forward to during those rather flat grey days after Christmas may be appreciated even more than yet another social occasion during the run-up to Christmas.

Annual reunions

Many retired employees greatly look forward to the regular yearly get-together with former work colleagues. As well as the meal, there is the opportunity to talk over old times and to catch up on current news and gossip. It is always sad when there are missing faces, but this can sometimes be avoided if the organiser tries to ensure that the journey is manageable by those people who are getting rather frail.

Changing rituals

While party members are frequently consulted regarding day outings, their opinions are often not sought concerning the form that annual reunions take. Often these follow a long-inherited pattern which may or may not suit people any more. The dubious argument that 'older people don't like change' is often put forward as a justification for not considering alternatives.

Changes can be for the better and at some point it may be relevant to rethink and reorder celebrations accordingly. Are speeches too long? Is the traditional menu rather too much for older appetites? Is the occasion too formal/informal?

Some organisations have stopped booking a private dinner in banqueting rooms in London, having found that, for the same price, they can enjoy not only a dinner but an inclusive overnight hotel stay at a seaside resort or country hotel – a good example of getting better value for money. All the problems of city parking plus getting home late at night are thus avoided; and there is the additional bonus that members have more time to spend together.

Often little extra touches such as floral table decorations or a small take-home gift can help make such annual occasions memorable. You may like to take advantage of the opportunity for a group photo, though this does not necessarily require the services of an outside professional photographer. The assignment could be handed over to a member of the party who is a good amateur photographer, or members can be encouraged to take their own pictures. A display of photographs from the previous year, and perhaps photos from a summer outing, can be put on show on a notice board.

OVERNIGHT STOPS

The immediate reaction of many group organisers to the idea of an overnight stop will be that it's simply not worth the extra trouble. This is even more likely to be the case since the new Package Travel Regulations, which affect any trip involving an overnight stay, were introduced at the end of 1992 (see pp 75–76).

There is, too, a practical economic disadvantage to a one-night-only stop in that the additional cost of a single night's accommodation is likely to be totally disproportionate to the overall cost of the outing. Many groups would rather opt for a mini-break of two to three days, which usually works out much better value for money. If you're going to stay in a hotel, you may as well have time to enjoy all the facilities, such as a swimming pool or sauna, as well as the advantage of a touring base.

If you do nevertheless decide to arrange an overnight stop, you will obviously need to check on party members' requirements before you book accommodation, for example:

- whether people are willing to share a room;
- whether they need a toilet en suite or very near the room;

- whether they need a room that is not up too many stairs;
- any special dietary needs.

Buying in a package from a commercial operator

One option is to buy in a package from a commercial operator. There is no shortage of London theatre packages, which is probably the kind of outing which most often involves an overnight stop. This eliminates most of the extra organisation and the anxiety about complying with the Package Travel Regulations, though it will still be the organiser's responsibility to check that the tour operator is complying with current Regulations.

In spite of the additional work entailed by the new Regulations, there is evidence that many organisers still prefer to 'shop around', putting together their own package of transport and accommodation to suit the particular needs of their party.

Accommodation options if you arrange your own package

Chains catering for groups include Hilton Hotels, Forte Travelodge, Friendly Hotels and Jarvis Hotels. These hotels can also be used for pre-booked meal stops en route.

It is also worth considering an independent private hotel, many of which advertise in the publication *Coaches Welcome* (details on p 88). 'We can only accommodate one coach but my word, don't we look after them' reads the advertisement for Rhos Abbey Hotel in North Wales.

Most hotels will offer a free night's stay for the driver/organiser of parties over a certain number. Some offer a free inspection night for the organiser.

University campus accommodation

The British Universities Accommodation Consortium (BUAC – address on p 82) produces an annual brochure; it also has an exhibition featuring the facilities of over 60 member universities. Some are available only over summer, Easter and Christmas periods; others offer accommodation all the year round. New upgraded student residences mean an increasing amount of en suite accommodation as well as better bathroom–bedroom ratios. Groups can opt for full board, half board, or bed and breakfast.

University accommodation has certain advantages over ordinary hotels:

- It is usually cheaper than hotel accommodation, particularly in central London and other city centres.

- There are lots of single rooms available, as most student accommodation consists of single study bedrooms. In addition, there is no single room supplement, as there is with hotels.

- As there are huge numbers of beds available, you might not have to book so far in advance. You may even get a booking at short notice, particularly if there is a conference cancellation.

The way arrangements are made is usually convenient for the group organiser. For any first booking, you will receive an invitation to inspect the venue. You will receive a detailed quotation on all the services you may wish to use at an early stage, which helps with the planning. When you book, a member of staff is nominated as your contact during your group's stay.

Deposits, confirmations and arrangements for payment vary from venue to venue.

For details of the new Package Travel Regulations and how they affect overnight stays, see pages 75–76.

Youth Hostel Accommodation

Parties of any age-group can use this budget-priced accommodation which is a useful option, particularly for an overnight stop in London. The Rotherhithe hostel in Docklands, for example, is purpose-built and has smaller than usual shared rooms.

Wherever you stay, individual membership is not necessary. Leaders will need to apply for a Group Organiser's Card for booking purposes. A *Youth Hostel Guide for Groups* is available from the Youth Hostels Association at the address on p 87.

8 Insurance and other legal requirements

However short the outing, things can always go wrong. One of your party could have an accident; valuables could be lost or stolen; a third party could be injured in an accident involving your coach or minibus; one of your party could cause damage by their actions. Proper insurance should cover you and your party against these and other eventualities.

This chapter covers the different types of insurance that may be required for day outings. It also looks at the new Package Travel Regulations and how they affect overnight stays.

INSURANCE FOR DAY OUTINGS

Different types of insurance may be needed for a day outing. If you belong to a club or other organisation, some or all of these may already be covered by their insurance. The insurance available to Age Concern affiliated groups from Alexander & Alexander UK Ltd, for example, includes public liability, employer's liability, personal accident and money. A group organiser may wish to confirm that the insurance carried by a club or organisation does cover outings as well as activities on the organisation's premises.

Some types of insurance such as personal belongings insurance may already be covered by party members' own personal household insurance. If this is the case, the organiser may not need to arrange extra insurance for the trip.

Public liability

Public liability insurance covers both the organisation's responsibility to other members of the party and their legal liability to the public at large for the actions of members of their party. Take the case where a group of people go for a country walk and the organiser fails to ensure that anyone shuts a gate. As a result animals get loose and stray on to a main road, causing a horrendous accident. The resulting insurance claims could amount to millions. The responsibility for closing the gate will normally rest with the individual. However, if the organisation is held to be legally liable, the policy cover will be operative.

Members of the party, including the group organiser, should be covered for public liability under their existing household insurance as far as their personal responsibility as individuals is concerned.

Because the risk of a claim under public liability insurance is small, premiums are usually correspondingly small. But it is vital to be insured because claims can involve very large sums of money.

Employer's liability

This provides compensation for employees for injury incurred in the course of their work for which the employer is held to be legally liable. The organiser should check that registered voluntary workers and committee members are covered as well as paid staff.

Personal belongings and personal accident

Organisers should remind people to make sure that any expensive items such as cameras, camcorders, binoculars, etc, are covered for 'all risks' under their own household contents insurance. 'All risks' means that items are covered when you take them out of the house as well as at home.

Personal accident insurance provides cover in case of an accident, such as falling when getting out of the coach or on the pavement.

The group organiser may wish to consider a day excursion insurance for their party from a company called Travellers' Protection Services (address on p 87). This covers accidental loss and/or theft of personal belongings and provides limited cover for personal accident. The company also specialises in insurance to meet the requirements of the 1992 Package Travel Regulations (see below).

Cancellation

This is usually not offered for day trips. Unlike a holiday, a day trip is unlikely to be cancelled at short notice. If individuals are sick, then their places will be taken by someone else if possible. Age Concern Insurance Services (address on p 82) does, however, offer a comprehensive holiday insurance which can be taken out for a single day and which covers cancellation.

Vehicle insurance

Any organiser using their own car on a trip needs to check that the insurance company allows people other than the named driver to drive the car, should the need arise.

A volunteer driver of a minibus should check whether the insurance company specifies any upper age limits and that they comply with any other criteria laid down in the organisation's vehicle insurance policy.

OVERNIGHT STOPS: THE NEW PACKAGE TRAVEL REGULATIONS

Any trip that includes an overnight stay or lasts longer than 24 hours could now be subject to the new Package Travel Regulations which came into effect at the end of 1992. These Regulations, which implement a European Community Directive, are aimed at wider consumer protection for the general public. They set out information which must be given to consumers, make the organiser liable to the consumer for the performance of the contract, require security for travellers' money and (in the case of trips abroad) guaranteed repatriation in case of insolvency.

The EC Directive does not distinguish between people who organise stays as part of their job and those who do so in a voluntary capacity. Anyone who arranges holidays, short breaks or overnight stays for a group of people may therefore fall within the scope of the Regulations. Day outings are not included, but an overnight stop after a theatre visit would be.

Copies of the *Package Travel, Package Holidays and Package Tours Regulations* (details on p 89) can be obtained from Her Majesty's Stationery Office. The Department of Trade and Industry has published free *Guidance Notes* (now revised – details on p 89) to be read in conjunction with the Regulations. These explain certain key terms, for example who might be defined as 'an organiser' and what constitutes 'a package'.

Nevertheless, there are still many grey areas which are open to different interpretations. 'Occasional' organisers may not be covered by the new Regulations, but what does 'occasional' mean? Does it depend on regularity or frequency? Although one legal opinion has suggested that an annual trip, being regular, could be subject to the new Regulations, the better view is probably that frequency is also relevant. On this basis a regular annual trip would probably be regarded as occasional. Only when cases have been tested in the courts will the ambiguities be clarified.

The first thing organisations need to do is to read the Package Travel Regulations very carefully in the light of their own circumstances. Decisions will then have to be made regarding any future plans for excursions involving an overnight stay. Much may depend to what extent a local club or group is backed by a larger umbrella organisation. If you are in doubt, you may find it helpful to contact your local Trading Standards Department (address in the local telephone directory). Trading Standards Officers are responsible for enforcing certain aspects of the Regulations and may be able to advise you.

A group may decide to accept new obligations, including the setting up of an independent trust account to safeguard members' contributions. An alternative, already mentioned on page 71, might be to buy in a ready-made package from a tour operator. In this case, the group organiser may be acting as the 'consumer' rather than the 'organiser' of a package. But the organiser would still need to check the claims being made by the tour operator.

9 The big day

The first thing everyone involved probably does on the morning of the day is to look out of the window to see what the weather is doing. Don't despair at dark clouds or rain – it seldom rains all day long, and it may well be fine, or at least dry, at your destination.

Television weather forecasts are not a lot of use because they tend to be far too general. Local commercial radio forecasts are better. Weathercall is a telephone service covering 27 different areas of the country, using information supplied by the Meteorological Office. For information see the *Thompson Directory* or *Yellow Pages*. Some newspapers run similar weather forecast services. You may even be able to make a prior arrangement with a contact near your destination whom you can telephone on the day.

But if the rain proves to be non-stop, and your planned venue is mainly outdoors, then you may have to fall back on a contingency plan, as suggested on page 45.

If you have planned carefully in advance, there shouldn't be much for you to do on the day except make sure all your arrangements run as smoothly as possible – and enjoy the outing.

WHAT TO TAKE WITH YOU

As part of your planning, you will probably have been compiling a list of things to bring with you on the day. Your list will probably include most of the following items:

- road map, in case you have to make a detour and the driver doesn't know an alternative route;
- phone numbers of all members of the party, including helpers;
- your schedule/itinerary for the day;
- list of contact phone numbers (for example the coach company, restaurants/cafes for meal stops, the venue, hospital, police, a base contact number);
- confirmation of all bookings plus receipts where relevant (coach, pre-booked meals, venue tickets, etc);
- phone cards (BT and Mercury), change for the telephone, and a mobile phone if you own or can borrow one (you can hire them for a day, but the cost might add an unacceptable amount to the overall cost of the trip – see the *Yellow Pages*);
- credit cards/cheque book and cash float;
- travel sickness pills;
- bottled water for swallowing pills and tablets;
- sick bags;
- wet wipes;
- first aid pack;
- spare umbrellas;
- music tapes (people's favourites for playing on the journey);
- plastic sacks for collecting up rubbish in the coach;
- a camera.

Group organiser 'If anyone is worried about travel sickness, I suggest they hold a 2p piece in each hand. It's supposed to work by magnetism. It's something I used to tell my five-year-olds when I was a playgroup leader, and it seems to work with any age group.'

MAKING SURE NO ONE GETS LOST

As people arrive at the pick-up point, you will obviously check them off against your list of party members, so that when you set off you know exactly who is with you. The following tips should help ensure that no one gets lost or separated from your party during the day:

- Always re-check numbers and do a roll call after each stop. Make sure everyone realises the importance of getting back to the coach at the agreed time, and understands exactly how long you are prepared to wait.
- The organiser should wear a bright easily identifiable colour which people can spot from a long distance away.
- Helpers, too, should wear readily identifiable clothing.
- Remind party members to learn to recognise the coach. One looks much the same as any other when they're all together in a huge parking area. Put a familiar mascot in the front or rear window of the coach, or put a big sign in the side window identifying your party.

A situation when it is particularly easy for people to get lost is when you are coming home in the dark and stop at a service station, especially the two-section kind linked by an overhead bridge, usually with identical facilities on each side. Everyone needs to be clear which side of the motorway they are on and in which direction they are travelling.

Another risky point is when the party is changing from one form of transport to another.

Group organiser 'Usually I say, keep a sense of direction and if you get lost, don't wander. When we went on a day trip to France, I told them that if they missed the coach to come through the passenger terminal and wait there.'

AFTER THE OUTING

Even when the outing is over, the group organiser's task is not quite done. It is always a good idea to make your own notes about the day while it is fresh in your mind – what went wrong, what was particularly successful, restaurants/pubs that you might like to visit on another occasion, what you would do differently another time.

You will also need to write thank-you letters to helpers – just a brief note to show your appreciation. If you found a restaurant, pub, hotel, coach company or whatever especially helpful and obliging, you may want to thank them too – especially if you think you might want to make use of them on a future occasion.

Two other things you may want to do are get feedback and get publicity.

Getting feedback

It is extremely useful to get feedback from the rest of the party. Anyone who has ever been on any kind of outing invariably has some comment to offer on how things could have been better. You can ask for feedback at the next meeting or through a questionnaire or more informally.

Age Concern group organiser 'I invite three or four people from the pop-in parlour who went on the outing back to my home for a cup of tea. That way I get feedback I wouldn't get otherwise and it keeps me in touch.'

This feedback shouldn't be taken as personal criticism of the organiser nor as a post mortem, but rather as potentially useful suggestions for future outings. You as the group organiser need to know that you are getting it right and giving members what they want.

Getting publicity

Sending a short news item about the outing – preferably with photos – to your local paper or to a company in-house journal may be a good idea for several reasons. Apart from anything else, most people will feel pleased to see their outing covered; it will be a final bit of enjoyment they can derive from the trip.

Usually someone who has been on the outing will be willing to write a short piece for you; if no one else can be persuaded, you can always write it yourself. If you want someone to take photos on the day, you will obviously need to arrange this in advance. Even if you don't manage to arrange any publicity about the trip, photos are certain to be appreciated.

As mentioned on page 43, sending an item to the local paper is a way of showing your appreciation if the trip was funded or partially funded by a sponsor such as the local Rotary Club. It will be good publicity for the organisation that made the donation, and may well help encourage both them and other organisations to make similar donations in the future. It will also be good publicity for your own group or organisation, possibly helping to attract new members, new helpers or even new offers of funding.

If the outing was organised by a company for its retired employees, an item in the in-house journal will again show your appreciation and encourage them to carry on providing outings in the future.

Further Information

USEFUL ADDRESSES

Age Concern Insurance Services
*Offers comprehensive travel insurance
which can be taken out for a single day.*

Garrod House
Chaldon Road
Caterham
Surrey CR3 5YZ
Tel: 0883 346964

ATS Travel Ltd
*Specialises in travel/day outings for
elderly and disabled people.*

ATS House
1 Tank Hill Road
Purfleet
Essex RM16 1SX
Tel: 0708 863198

BBC Radio Ticket Unit
*For tickets for BBC Radio
audience shows.*

Broadcasting House
Portland Place
London W1A 1AA

BBC Television Ticket Unit
*For tickets for BBC Television
audience shows.*

Television Centre
Wood Lane
London W12 7SB

**British Universities Accommodation
Consortium (BUAC)**
*Publishes a group guide to
accommodation in universities,
and holds an annual exhibition.*

FREEPOST
Box No 1025
University Park
Nottingham NG7 2RD
Tel: 0602 504571

Can Be Done Ltd
Specialises in travel/day outings
for elderly and disabled people.

7–11 Kensington High Street
London W8 5NP
Tel: 081-907 2400

Community Transport Association
Publishes handbook and runs courses
on handling wheelchairs, passenger
assistance and disability awareness.
Advises on minibuses and specially
adapted vehicles.

Highbank
Halton Street
Hyde
Cheshire SK14 2NY
Tel: 061-351 1475/061-366 6685

Crusader Group Travel
Agency run by National Express for
local approved coach companies.

Room 229
Ashdown House
Gatwick Airport
West Sussex RH6 0JH
Tel: 0345 581185
(countrywide number
charged at local rates)

Disabled Living
Organises day outings for
disabled people.

4 St Chad's Street
Cheetham
Manchester M8 8QA
Tel: 061-832 3678

English Heritage
Publishes an annual guide to its
properties and a free booklet
for disabled visitors.

Fortress House
23 Savile Row
London W1X 1AB
Tel: 071-973 3000

Farm Shop and Pick Your Own
Association (FSPA)
For a free booklet listing 'pick your
own' farms throughout the UK. Send
a large sae.

Agricultural House
Knightsbridge
London SW1X 7NJ
Tel: 071-235 5077

Group Sales Box Office
For group bookings for
West End theatres.

4 Norris Street
London SW1Y 4RJ
Tel: 071-930 6123

Guild of Master Caterers
*Promotes Mature Choice scheme –
manageable meals at reduced prices
for the over-50s.*

Guild House
Lloyds Bank Chambers
71–73 High Street
Stone
Staffordshire ST15 8AG
Tel: 0785 811822

**ICHF (International Craft
and Hobby Fair) Ltd**
*Organises three regular crafts exhibitions:
Creative Stitches, Sewing for Pleasure
and Crafts Alive. Leaflets giving
forthcoming venues and dates available.*

Dominic House
Seaton Road
Highcliffe
Dorset BH23 5HW
Tel: 0425 272711

**Independent Television
Commission (ITC)**
*For addresses of regional
ITV companies.*

Information Office
33 Foley Street
London W1P 7LB
Tel: 071-824 7756

**Metropolitan Police Coach
Advisory Service**
*For advice about setting down and
picking up points for coaches in London.*

Tintagel House
Albert Embankment
London SE1 7TT
Tel: 071-230 5332

National Trust
*Publishes an annual handbook about
its properties, and a leaflet for
disabled visitors.*

36 Queen Anne's Gate
London SW1H 9AS
Tel: 071-222 9251

National Trust for Scotland

5 Charlotte Square
Edinburgh EH2 4DU
Tel: 031-226 5922

Ramblers' Association
*For addresses of local Ramblers'
Association groups, who might be able
to provide volunteer guides for walks.*

1–5 Wandsworth Road
London SW8 2XX
Tel: 071-582 6878

Royal Horticultural Society (RHS)
*For information about RHS gardens
and flower shows.*

Wisley
Woking
Surrey GU23 6QB
Tel: 0483 224234

**Royal Society for Disability and
Rehabilitation (RADAR)**
*Publishes access guides for various
types of venue. Write to them for their
list of publications.*

25 Mortimer Street
London W1N 8AB
Tel: 071-637 5400

Society of West End Theatres
Publishes a Disabled Access Guide *and
a monthly* Group Sales Bulletin.
*Exhibition Stagefair is an annual trade
fair for group organisers.*

Bedford Chambers
The Piazza
Covent Garden
London WC2E 8HQ
Tel: 071-836 3193

Tourist boards

English Tourist Board

Thames Tower
Blacks Road
London W6
Tel: 081-846 9000

Scottish Tourist Board

23 Ravelston Terrace
Edinburgh EH4 3EU
Tel: 031-332 2433

Wales Tourist Board

Brunel House
2 Fitzalan Road
Cardiff CF1 1YZ
Tel: 0222 499909

Cumbria Tourist Board
Covers Cumbria.

Ashleigh
Holly Road
Windermere
Cumbria LA23 2AQ
Tel: 05394 44444

East Anglia Tourist Board
*Covers Cambridgeshire, Essex,
Norfolk and Suffolk.*

Toppesfield Hall
Hadleigh
Suffolk IP7 5DN
Tel: 0473 822922

East Midlands Tourist Board
Covers Derbyshire, Leicestershire,
Lincolnshire, Northamptonshire
and Nottinghamshire.

Exchequergate
Lincoln
Lincolnshire LN2 1PZ
Tel: 0522 531521

Heart of England Tourist Board
Covers Gloucestershire, Hereford and
Worcester, Shropshire, Staffordshire,
Warwickshire and West Midlands.

Woodside
Larkhill Road
Worcester
Worcestershire WR5 2EF
Tel: 0905 763436

London Tourist Board
Covers the Greater London area.

26 Grosvenor Gardens
London SW1W 0DU
Tel: 071-730 3450

North West Tourist Board
Covers Cheshire, Greater Manchester,
Lancashire, Merseyside and the High
Peak District of Derbyshire.

Swan House
Swan Meadow Road
Wigan Pier
Wigan
Lancashire WN3 5BB
Tel: 0942 821222

Northumbria Tourist Board
Covers Cleveland, Durham,
Northumberland, and Tyne and Wear.

Aykley Heads
Durham DH1 5UX
Tel: 091-384 6905

South East England Tourist Board
Covers East and West Sussex,
Kent and Surrey.

The Old Brew House
Warwick Park
Tunbridge Wells
Kent TN2 5TU
Tel: 0892 540766

Southern Tourist Board
Covers eastern and northern Dorset,
Hampshire and Isle of Wight.

40 Chamberlayne Road
Eastleigh
Hants SO5 5JH
Tel: 0703 620006

West Country Tourist Board
Covers Avon, Cornwall, Devon, parts
of Dorset, Somerset, Wiltshire and
Isles of Scilly.

60 St David's Hill
Exeter
Devon EX4 4SY
Tel: 0392 76351

Yorkshire & Humberside Tourist Board
Covers Humberside, North Yorkshire,
South Yorkshire and West Yorkshire.

312 Tadcaster Road
York YO2 2HF
Tel: 0904 707961

Travellers' Protection Services Ltd
Offers personal belongings and personal
accident insurance for day outings, plus
insurance to meet the requirements of
the new Package Travel Regulations.

82 Upper St Giles Street
Norwich
Norfolk NR2 1LT
Tel: 0603 767699

Tripscope
Advises on journey planning for
individual disabled people nationwide.

The Court Yard
Evelyn Road
London W4 5JL
Tel: 081-994 9294

Youth Hostels Association
Publishes an annual guide for
group accommodation.

Trevelyan House
St Stephen's Hill
St Albans
Herts AL1 2DY
Tel: 0727 845047

Useful publications

Coaches Welcome, free annual publication with specialist information for groups, including meal stops and private hotels. From Lewis Productions Ltd, Unit 3, River Gardens Business Centre, Spur Road, Feltham, Middlesex TW14 0SN. Tel: 081-890 1111.

Community Transport Manual on Driver Assessment and Training, available from the Community Transport Association (address on p 83).

Disabled Access Guide, listing facilities at West End theatres, available free from the Society of West End Theatres (address on p 85); enclose an sae with a 36p stamp. They also publish a monthly *Group Sales Bulletin*.

Factory Shop Guides, regularly updated, available through bookshops or from Gillian Cutress, 34 Park Hill, London SW4 9PB. Tel: 071-622 3722. There is also a leaflet listing regions covered and prices – enclose an sae.

First Aid Manual, published by St John Ambulance, St Andrews Ambulance Association and the British Red Cross. Available from good bookshops or from St John Ambulance Supplies Department, Priory House, St John's Lane, London EC1M 4DA. 071-251 2482/0004. Price £7.99.

Gardens of England and Wales, annual publication on gardens open to the public, often known as 'the Yellow Book'. Available through booksellers or by post from the National Gardens Scheme, Hatchlands Park, East Clanden, Guildford, Surrey GU4 7RT. Tel: 0483 211535. Price £3.

Group Travel Organiser, invaluable monthly magazine for people involved in arranging outings, free to nominated organisers. Write to Quadrant House, 250 Kennington Lane, London SE11 5RD. Tel: 071-735 5058.

Guide to English Heritage Properties, free to English Heritage members, and otherwise obtainable from English Heritage Postal Sales, PO Box 229, Northampton NN6 9RY. Tel: 0604 781163. Price £3.25. They also publish a free guide for disabled visitors.

London for the Travel Trade, free from the London Tourist Board (address on p 86).

Museums and Galleries of Great Britain, annual publication on sale in major bookshops or from Reed Information Services, Windsor Court, East Grinstead House, East Grinstead, West Sussex RH19 1XA. Tel: 0342 326972. Price £6.90.

National Trust Gardens Handbook, describing over 140 Trust gardens, available from the National Trust (address on p 84). Price £3.95.

National Trust Handbook, listing all their properties, available from the National Trust (address on p 84). Price £3.95. They also publish a free guide for disabled visitors.

National Trust Historic Houses Handbook, describing all the Trust houses open to the public, available from the National Trust (address on p 84). Price £4.50.

Package Travel, Package Holidays and Package Tours Regulations (1992, SI 1992/3288), available from HMSO Publications Centre, PO Box 276, London SW8 5DT. Tel: 071-873 0011 (enquiries); 071-873 9090 (orders). Price £3.10. *Guidance Notes* to be read in conjunction with the Package Travel Regulations, free from the Department of Trade and Industry, Consumers Affairs Division, Room 414, 10–18 Victoria Street, London SW1H 0NN. Tel: 071-215 3338.

Package Travel Regulations: A practical guide by Peter B Rogers, published by Landor Travel Publications, Quadrant House, 250 Kennington Lane, London SE11 5RD. Tel: 071-582 3872. Price £16.95.

Places that Care – An access guide to places of interest for elderly and disabled people, compiled by Michael B Yarrow. Available from Mediair Marketing Services, 72 High Street, Poole, Dorset BH15 1DA. Tel: 0202 671545. Price £5.99 inc p & p.

Practical First Aid, new revised edition, published by the British Red Cross/Dorling Kindersley. Price £4.99.

Sports Centres for Disabled People and other access guides published by RADAR (address on p 85).

About Age Concern

Arranging Outings for Older People: A group organiser's guide is one of a wide range of publications produced by Age Concern England – National Council on Ageing. In addition, Age Concern is actively engaged in training, information provision, research and campaigning for retired people and those who work with them. It is a registered charity dependent on public support for the continuation of its work.

Age Concern England links closely with Age Concern centres in Scotland, Wales and Northern Ireland to form a network of over 1,400 independent local UK groups. These groups, with the invaluable help of an estimated 250,000 volunteers, aim to improve the quality of life for older people and develop services appropriate to local needs and resources. These include advice and information, day care, visiting services, transport schemes, clubs, and specialist facilities for physically and mentally frail older people.

Age Concern England
1268 London Road
London SW16 4ER
Tel: 081-679 8000

Age Concern Scotland
54a Fountainbridge
Edinburgh EH3 9PT
Tel: 031-228 5656

Age Concern Wales
4th Floor
1 Cathedral Road
Cardiff CF1 9SD
Tel: 0222 371566

Age Concern Northern Ireland
3 Lower Crescent
Belfast BT7 1NR
Tel: 0232 245729

Publications from ◆A◆C◆E◆Books

A wide range of titles is published by Age Concern England under the ACE Books imprint.

General

An Active Retirement
Nancy Tuft
Bursting with information on hobbies, sports, educational opportunities and voluntary work, this practical guide is ideal for retired people seeking new ways to fill their time but uncertain where to start.

£7.95   0–86242–119–5

Living, Loving and Ageing: Sexual and personal relationships in later life
Wendy Greengross and Sally Greengross
Sexuality is often regarded as the preserve of the younger generation. At last, here is a book for older people, and those who work with them, which tackles the issues in a straightforward fashion, avoiding preconceptions and bias.

£4.95   0–86242–070–9

Eating Well on a Budget
Sara Lewis
Completely revised, the new edition of this successful title offers sound advice on shopping and cooking cost-effectively and includes wholesome original recipes for four complete weekly menus.

£5.95   0–86242–120–9

Working with Older Volunteers: A practical guide
Alan Dingle

Older volunteers form a valuable resource available to many groups in need of support, yet often offers of help are not tapped to their full potential. This book is designed for use by those responsible for recruiting, placing and motivating older volunteers and is full of practical advice and suggestions.

For further information please telephone 081-679 8000.

Money Matters

Your Rights: A guide to money benefits for older people
Sally West

A highly acclaimed annual guide to the State benefits available to older people. Contains current information on Income Support, Housing Benefit and the State Retirement Pension, among other matters, and includes advice on how to claim them.

For further information please telephone 081-679 8000.

Earning Money in Retirement
Kenneth Lysons

Many people, for a variety of reasons, wish to continue in some form of paid employment beyond the normal retirement age. This helpful guide explores the practical implications of such a choice and highlights some of the opportunities available.

£5.95   0–86242–103–9

Health and Care

Know Your Medicines
Pat Blair
Sponsored by Esso UK plc

We would all like to know more about the medicines we take. The second edition of this successful guide is written for older people and their carers and examines how the body works and the effects of medication.

£6.95   0–86242–100–4

The Community Care Handbook: The new system explained
Barbara Meredith

The provision of care in the community is changing as a result of recent legislation. Written by one of the country's foremost experts, this book explains the background to the reforms, what they are, how they will work and who they will affect.

£11.95   0–86242–121–7

Your Health in Retirement
Dr J A Muir Gray and Pat Blair

This book is a comprehensive source of information to help readers look after themselves and work towards better health. Produced in an easy-to-read A–Z style, full details are given of people and useful organisations from which advice and assistance can be sought.

£4.50   0–86242–082–2

To order books, send a cheque or money order, payable to Age Concern England, to the address below. Postage and packing are free. Credit card orders may be made on 081-679 8000.

Age Concern England (DEPT C)
PO Box 9
London SW16 4EX

SERVICE-RELATED BOOKLETS FROM AGE CONCERN

Community Care Changes
A series of five booklets on aspects of community care legislation and how to help your organisation thoroughly address these issues, £17 for the set or:

Complaints £1.95
Community Care Plans £2.75
Quality and Inspection £5.00
Purchasing and Contracting £5.00
Assessment and Care Management £5.00

Information is presented through a question and answer format.

Contracts and the Contract Culture
An introductory guide to assess the pros and cons of contracting for voluntary organisations and the questions you need to ask yourselves and the potential contractor. £5.00

Speak up for Yourself
Aims to provide a basic understanding of what advocacy means and to outline how the philosophy may be reflected in practice. £2.00

Standards in Day Care Services
Covers a range of services related to day care and how standards can be set and monitored. £7.50

Orders under £10 for service-related booklets should include a cheque payable to Age Concern England. Orders over £10 can be invoiced.

For further information or to order any of the above booklets, contact:

Fieldwork Services Unit
Age Concern England
1268 London Road
London SW16 4ER
Tel: 081-679 8000 ext 2304

INFORMATION FACTSHEETS

Age Concern England produces over 30 factsheets on a variety of subjects. Among these the following titles may be of interest to readers of this book:

Factsheet 4 *Holidays for older people*
Factsheet 26 *Travel information for older people*
Factsheet 30 *Leisure education*

To order factsheets

Single copies are available free on receipt of a 9″ × 6″ sae. If you require a selection of factsheets or multiple copies totalling more than five, charges will be given on request.

A complete set of factsheets is available in a ring binder at the current cost of £34, which includes the first year's subscription. The current cost for annual subscription for subsequent years is £14. There are different rates of subscription for people living abroad.

Factsheets are revised and updated throughout the year and membership of the subscription service will ensure that your information is always current.

For further information, or to order factsheets, write to:

Information and Policy Department
Age Concern England
1268 London Road
London SW16 4ER